STIRLING CASTLE

Th

For my mother, and in memory of my father

HISTORIC SCOTLAND

STIRLING CASTLE

RICHARD FAWCETT

B. T. Batsford Ltd / Historic Scotland

First published 1995

Typeset by Bernard Cavender Design & Greenwood Graphics Publishing
and printed in Great Britain by The Bath Press, Bath

Published by B. T. Batsford Ltd
4 Fitzhardinge Street, London W1H 0AH

A CIP catalogue record for this book is available from
the British Library

ISBN 0 7134 7623 0 (limp)
0 7134 7622 2 (cased)

Contents

Illustrations

Colour Plates

Acknowledgements

My warmest thanks are due to the Earl of Mar and Kellie, Mr Iain MacIvor, Mr John Dunbar and Professor Geoffrey Barrow. The first of those, who is the Hereditary Keeper of the castle, generously agreed to write the Foreword to this small volume, while the researches of the others provided a firm foundation for parts of what I have written. They have also read through the text and helped me greatly with their advice. I am very grateful to several others who were similarly prepared to read the text, in whole or in part, and to aid my task with their views, though I must accept responsibility for the opinions expressed. These included Dr David Breeze, Mrs Doreen Grove, Dr Noel Fojut, the late Mr Iain Malcolm, Dr Aonghus MacKechnie, Mr Duncan Peet and, as always, my wife. My thanks are gratefully proffered to Gordon Ewart and his colleagues in Kirkdale Archaeology for the enthusiasm they have put into excavations at the castle over recent years, and for discussion of their findings with me. For preparing the plans my gratitude is due to Mrs Sylvia Stevenson. For much help in photographic matters I owe thanks to Mr David Henrie; unless otherwise stated in the captions, all photographs are copyright Historic Scotland.

Foreword

By the Earl of Mar and Kellie
Hereditary Keeper of Stirling Castle

Stirling Castle is one of Scotland's most significant sites, from the past, at the present and for the future. Set on a volcanic rock at one of the most strategic locations in Scotland, it was inevitable that fortifications would be raised here as men sought to establish order in the developing Scotland. As this began to be achieved, new and artistic ideas were implemented, giving to posterity the structures that we can now enjoy. Stirling Castle continues to develop and find new uses for its enclosed and open spaces. Today we can add to our understanding of what happened at this castle and how it helped to shape the Scottish nation.

Dr Fawcett's text brings to life the long-running, continuing drama that has been enacted at Stirling Castle. His academic precision and interpretative flair have improved my knowledge of this castle, and I'm sure they will for you too.

Mar and Kellie
Hereditary Keeper
October 1994

Introduction

Stirling Castle, set virtually at the central point of the Scottish kingdom, and on a site which may well have been fortified since prehistoric times, is a remarkable survival. Throughout the Middle Ages and the period of the Renaissance, from the time when it first comes on record in the early twelfth century, it was one of the most important royal castles. It played a particularly significant role in the wearisomely long wars with England that erupted from the 1290s onwards, as a result of Edward I's attempts to dominate and eventually to annex Scotland, after he had been called in to adjudicate between the various claimants to the throne. In the course of those wars the castle changed hands on a number of occasions. The attempt by Edward II's forces to relieve its English garrison in 1314, and their consequent defeat by Robert I at the battle of Bannockburn (see 7), would alone give it a permanent place in history. While no visitors who wish to enjoy the castle's full flavour should allow themselves to forget the events of those Wars of Independence, however, it is not those events that are reflected in the extraordinary complex of structures that make up the castle. The core of what is now seen is a group of buildings that provided a setting for the royal court of Stewart Scotland at its most brilliant period, in the reigns of James IV, James V, Mary Queen of Scots and James VI.

Observant visitors will quickly spot that the planning of the main royal enclave of the castle shows many parallels with that of Edinburgh Castle in the way the principal buildings are ranged around a roughly rectangular area on the highest part of the main enclosure (see **colour plate 3**) (though Stirling has, in addition, a highly impressive defensive forework across the main approach to the castle). There is a further close similarity between the two castles in their setting on naturally formidable volcanic-rock sites. Two factors, however, help to give Stirling its exceptional architectural interest. In the first place, a number of its buildings were conceived on a more magnificent scale than those at any other Scottish royal residence. In the second place, many of Stirling's buildings have been less completely remodelled than elsewhere and now present a more authentic impression of the splendours of the Scottish court in the later Middle Ages and the early Renaissance period.

But Stirling's interest extends beyond its royal buildings. Artillery defences that were probably built around the 1550s by Mary of Guise, on behalf of her absent daughter Mary Queen of Scots, who was queen of France as well as of Scotland, are now known to have survived more extensively than had been realized (see **46**). As such, they represent the most complete example to survive on Scottish soil of an early stone-built artillery fortification in the Italian style. In this they provide a foretaste of Stirling's future, in which purely military requirements were to become dominant. This was to be increasingly the case after James VI's accession to the English throne in 1603, but especially after the union of the two kingdoms in 1707, when extensive restructuring of the outer defences was carried out between 1708 and 1714. Indeed, the castle continued to serve as a military depot until as late as 1964, being continually modified to meet developing needs.

Together, all of the successive building operations which produced the Stirling Castle we now see offer a fascinating composite picture of how a major fortress and royal residence could be adapted to meet the diverse and changing functions it accommodated. Both the buildings and the history of the castle will be discussed in the following pages. But it is important not to see the castle in isolation, and at Stirling we are fortunate that many other buildings survive to help us appreciate its wider context. Among these are several medieval buildings, including the bridge at this most important crossing of the Forth (see **90**), the great parish church of the burgh (see **92**), and the royal abbey of Cambuskenneth (see **94**). Stirling also has the two best surviving examples of aristocratic town houses in Scotland, on the approaches to its castle, Mar's Work (see **95**), and Argyll's Lodging (see **97**), which vividly remind us of the central role played by the royal residences in the structure of medieval and Renaissance society. Except for the great parish church, which is happily still in use for worship, most of these buildings are cared for by the State through Historic Scotland, and they are briefly described and illustrated in the final chapter of the book.

CHAPTER ONE

Rock and fortress

The castle rock

It would be hard to think of a site anywhere else in Scotland that was a better candidate for fortification than that of Stirling Castle (**1, colour plates 1, 2, 3**). The combination of a superbly strong rock summit and a position virtually at the physical centre of the nation, overlooking the junction of several of the principal lines of communication across the country, gave Stirling a unique strategic value. Whoever commanded this site was well placed to control traffic both across the Midland valley and between the Lowlands and the Highlands, and this was amply reflected in the prominent place that Stirling came to occupy in Scotland's history. Indeed, its situation between the south and north, at the very heart of the country, led to the coining of the apt description of the rock as a brooch which held the parts of the country together. Nevertheless, it should not be assumed that fortifying such a

1 *Stirling Castle from the south-west.*

2 A view along the west face of the King's Old Building and the edge of the castle rock.

site can ever have been easy, since the great length of its perimeter meant that any attempt at fortification called for enormous technical and financial resources.

The rock which underlies the castle is the edge of what is known as a great sill, a thick layer of quartz-dolerite which spread out when still molten from a distant volcanic fissure in the earth's crust, about 350 million years ago. It forced its way horizontally beneath sedimentary rocks, which have since been stripped away by millions of years of erosion. The hard igneous rock has thus been revealed at a number of places, while at the same time the rocks have tilted, tipping the north-western edge of the sill upwards. This sill, which bears comparison with the great whin sill of northern England, along which Hadrian's Wall runs for much of its length, is also to be seen at Kirk o' Shotts, at Torphichen and at North Queensferry, as well as in central and north-eastern Fife.

By the beginning of the last Ice Age the castle rock may already have been a free-standing hill. But the movement of the ice-sheet which passed over the Stirling area, moving from south-west to south-east, removed the softer surrounding sediments and carved away the north and west faces of the hill. This exposed the hard dolerite in the form of vertical faces (2). Since the castle rock was an immovable obstacle within the flowing ice, this encouraged the preservation of the softer sediments downstream to the south-east. The tail, or tapering ramp, so formed was in time to provide the natural line of approach to the castle, and it was along this that the medieval burgh developed. Late in the Ice Age, the castle rock, which by then looked much as we now see it, stood high above a shallow inlet of the sea, in which sediments brought down by the Forth and other rivers accumulated in deep beds of clay. As the sea-level fell relative to the land, and the ice melted, deep peat beds built up on these carse clays, creating a wasteland of inhospitable marshes. This area embraced the Flanders, Blairdrummond and Drip Mosses, through which the Forth meandered eastwards to the retreating sea.

On each side of Stirling the river valley was restricted by hills: by the Ochils to the north-east, and to the south-west by the Gargunnock and Touch Hills. West of the Ochils the tributaries of the River Teith and Allan Water flowed down Strathyre and Strathallan respectively, meeting the Forth a little to the west of Stirling. Since the progressive draining of the marshes in recent centuries to create excellent level farmland, and the subsequent construction of a network of roads and railways across the area, it is difficult to imagine the restrictions that such a terrain once imposed on

travellers (3). But it must always be remembered that, although there was another crossing of the Forth for land traffic between the Flanders and Blairdrummond Mosses – at least for those who knew the area well enough – the crossing at Stirling must always have been the best. This was especially so since Stirling was not only at the lowest crossable point of the Forth, but was also at its highest navigable and tidal point, and was therefore accessible for seagoing vessels.

The earliest castle

Taking account of all this, it seems probable that the rock at Stirling must have been fortified over a very long period. It must be said at the outset, however, that we know nothing for certain about the history of the site before the early twelfth century. Indeed, although surviving records refer to an increasing amount of building from then onwards, it is not until about 1500 that we can begin to relate those records with certainty to the majority of the

3 The plains stretching out to the west of the castle, which are now fertile farmland but which used to be largely impassable marsh.

existing buildings. Nevertheless, it is interesting to speculate on some of the possibilities, though it must be stressed that much of what is said in this chapter about the early use of the site, and about the buildings likely to have been associated with it, is tentative. It seems likely, for example, that so prominent a site was occupied from prehistoric times, particularly since traces of early forts have been either found or postulated on a number of surrounding hills, including the slightly lower Gowan Hill immediately to east of the castle rock. However, no such settlement has so far been identified on the castle rock itself, though the areas of its surface that have been excavated to modern standards are relatively small, and evidence may yet be found.

Moving on in time, it was long thought likely that the main Roman road to the north must have crossed the Forth close to Stirling, and that there would thus have been a fort near the crossing. It also used to be thought that an inscribed stone on Gowan Hill was of Roman date. However, this stone is now known not to be so early, while the recent discovery of a fort higher up the valley at Doune suggests the line of the Roman road probably passed through there instead. This does not entirely preclude the possibility that a later fort was constructed near Stirling, and it should be mentioned that a small number of Roman coins have been found around the town. But it is perhaps more likely that these coins were from a native site, occupied by people who had obtained the coins in the course of trading with the Romans, and no traces of any fort have so far been found.

It is a slightly stronger possibility that one of the tribes known to the Romans fortified the rock. One of those tribes, the Maeatae, probably held land in the area, since a few miles to the north-east of Stirling there is a fort on the hill known as Dumyat, a name that is thought to mean 'fort of the Maeatae'. But it is perhaps even more likely that the castle rock was the main place of strength of the successors of another tribe, the Votadini, in the northern part of their territory. Those successors of the Votadini, who emerge in the early historical records as the people known as the Gododdin, are generally assumed to have had their main administrative centres at the castle rock in Edinburgh and at Traprain Law in East Lothian. It has been argued by some scholars, however, that Stirling could have been the chief settlement of an outlying enclave to the north-west of the main area under their control. This enclave was known as Manaw Gododdin, from which Clackmannan and Slamannan later took their names. It has also been suggested that Stirling is identifiable with a settlement referred to in the seventh and eighth centuries as Urbs Iudeu or Giudi.

While we are unlikely ever to know with certainty if Stirling was a stronghold of the Gododdin, by the seventh century the area was probably coming increasingly under the control of the Anglians of Northumbria, in north-eastern England. The Anglians were at that time intent on expanding northwards and we know, for example, that in 654 King Penda of Mercia (in central England) pursued Oswy, the Anglian king of the part of Northumbria known as Bernicia, as far as the place known as Iudeu. If Stirling was indeed identifiable with Iudeu, this could suggest it had become one of the centres of Oswy's authority. However, to add a further measure of confusion, Anglian control over the area north of the Forth–Clyde basin was itself almost certainly soon to be pushed back as a result of the defeat in 685 of the Anglian King Ecgfrith by King Brude at the battle of Nechtansmere. The latter was the ruler of the native Celtic peoples known as the Picts who occupied the area of Scotland north of the Forth that was sometimes known as Fortriu.

If we know little of Stirling in the times that the area was dominated by the Britons and Anglians, we know hardly more about it in the period that the Picts came increasingly under the sway of the Scots around the mid-ninth century. (For those unfamiliar with early Scottish history it should be said that, although it is from the people known as the Scots that Scotland takes its name, they had, in fact, originated in Ireland, and had only started to settle in an area centred on Argyll from around the year 500.) In the history of Scotland that he published in 1527, Hector Boece of King's College Aberdeen said that a castle at Stirling had been besieged by Kenneth mac Alpin. Kenneth had become king of the Scots in 842, and under his rule his people spread eastwards as a first stage on the long road towards creating a unified nation. It is certainly possible that, as suggested by Boece, Kenneth would have had to gain control of Stirling as he extended his rule across Pictland, though we have no confirmation of this from other sources. Somewhat later, Stirling also seems to figure in the rather puzzling prophecies attributed to the

Irish seer called Berchan. For the period corresponding to the reign of Constantine III (995–7), Berchan appears to have prophesied that there would be an unfortunate king who would be involved in battles from Stirling to Abertay; if nothing else, at least this may suggest that Stirling was regarded as a place of importance at that time.

The twelfth and thirteenth centuries

With the opening of the twelfth century we begin to enter a period when we know about historical events associated with the castle with a greater degree of certainty. At a date probably between 1107 and 1115 Alexander I arranged to have a chapel within the castle dedicated, and made provision for its endowments. From this we may reasonably assume there was a well-established royal castle here by the early twelfth century, possibly on the very highest point of the rock around the area where the present Chapel Royal and the King's Old

Building now come together. That castle must already have been one of the principal royal residences, since it is thought to have been within its walls that Alexander died in 1124. Alexander's chapel was possibly similar to the surviving chapel now associated with the name of St Margaret which was built within Edinburgh Castle by David I a few years later. Yet, if the Stirling chapel was of stone, it is very likely that the defensive walls and other buildings of the castle were still largely of timber, with thatched or turf roofs (**4**).

The growing importance of Stirling, and by implication also that of the royal castle, becomes increasingly clear as the twelfth century advances. The number of royal acts issued either from Stirling or from places in its vicinity in this century could even suggest that Stirling was at that time the main centre for the administration of the royal finances. It is

4 *A conjectural reconstruction sketch of the castle as it may have appeared in the earlier twelfth century (David Pollock).*

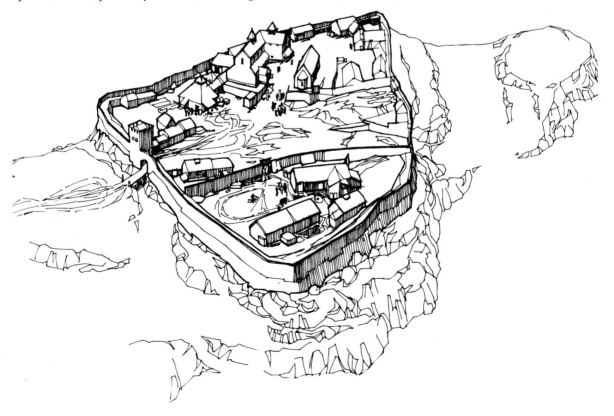

particularly during the reign of Alexander I's younger brother and successor, David I (1124–53), that we begin to see the care with which Scotland's kings were developing the area around their castle to provide an appropriate ambience for their court. At this phase of Scotland's history, it should be remembered, the country had no single capital in the modern sense: kings were expected to travel around their kingdom and the effective capital was wherever the king chose to be. But Stirling had evidently become one of the most important places in the kingdom. Soon after David's accession the settlement which was growing up on the approaches to the castle at Stirling was being referred to as one of the king's burghs, showing that it enjoyed the special privileges which it was hoped would encourage its development as a centre of trading activity. It was to remain one of the most prominent of such burghs throughout the Middle Ages.

David, who was Scotland's most pious king and later came to be widely regarded as a saint, was as deeply concerned with the spiritual as with the material welfare of his kingdom, and did much to encourage the reorganization of the Church on the pattern that was becoming usual in the rest of Europe. Naturally enough, we see evidence for this around his favourite residences. By about 1150 there were references to two churches within Stirling, one of which was probably the chapel in the castle, while the other was presumably the predecessor of the parish church of the Holy Rude, on the slopes below the castle. Some time around 1140 David also founded a major abbey of canons below the castle walls, in a loop of the River Forth at Cambuskenneth. In all of this there are close similarities with what he was doing at Edinburgh, with Cambuskenneth providing a parallel for Holyrood Abbey, and Holy Rude a parallel for St Giles' in Edinburgh. This should remind us that Edinburgh and Stirling were regarded as being of comparable importance. Nevertheless, there were other royal residences of this period where there was a similarly close relationship between the castle and a nearby abbey, as at Roxburgh in the Borders, where David brought Tironensian monks from Selkirk to a new abbey at Kelso.

For all his piety, David enjoyed the kingly sport of hunting, and it is during his reign that there are the first references to the forest of Stirling. It should be remembered in this context, of course, that 'forest' means a tract of land set aside for the chase rather than an area necessarily covered by trees.

The castle continued to be prominent during the reign of William I (the Lion, 1165–1214), the second of David I's grandsons to follow him to the throne. During William's reign part of the hunting forest mentioned above was enclosed to form a royal park, the first that is known of in Scotland, and a further confirmation of the favoured status of Stirling. However, it was also in his reign that the castle had to be first resigned into English hands. In an attempt to regain territory that he considered to be rightfully his, in 1174 William invaded England during an absence of Henry II in France. He was taken by surprise at Alnwick and carried ignominiously in shackles before Henry at Northampton. As the price of his freedom, under the terms of the Treaty of Falaise he had to accept Henry's overlordship of Scotland and was also forced to place his castles at Stirling, Edinburgh, Roxburgh, Berwick and Jedburgh under the English king's control. There is, however, no evidence that Stirling was ever occupied by the English at this time, and in 1189 he at last obtained the agreement of Richard I that the humiliating terms of the treaty should be overturned. Despite this disgrace, Stirling clearly continued to be one of William's favourite residences, and it was there that he died in 1214, his body being afterwards taken away to his new abbey at Arbroath for burial.

Later in the thirteenth century we read of what must have been significant building operations among the earliest of the Exchequer Rolls to have come down to us, and in 1287, for example, work was being carried out by Richard the master mason. Nothing of this is recognizable today, though traces of what could be an early curtain wall were found by excavation in 1994 in the gardens behind the Chapel Royal. This work was at the beginning of the traumatic period that followed the accidental death of Alexander III along the coast between Burntisland and Kinghorn in Fife in 1286. It was around the time this building work was under way that Alexander's widowed second queen, Yolande de Dreux, was resident within the castle, and for a while she claimed to be pregnant with a child of the king. The Lanercost chronicle suggests that she even attempted to foist an actor's son on the kingdom as being the product of their union. Once her claims were found to be false, the crown was inherited by Margaret, the 'Maid of Norway', Alexander's infant granddaughter by his first marriage, and the daughter of King Erik of Norway. She, however, died on her way to Scotland, probably on 26 September 1290, leaving no other undisputed claimant to the throne.

Stirling and the first phase of the Wars of Independence

Even before the Maid was sent for, it had been necessary to try to ensure that Edward I of England would not interfere with her right to succeed as queen of Scotland. Edward was the late king's brother-in-law as well as the Maid's nearest male relative after her father, and he was known still to maintain those claims to be overlord of Scotland that had been seen in William the Lion's dealings with Henry II. In July 1290, as part of an attempt to ensure stability, it had been agreed that the Maid should be betrothed to Edward's own heir, though the continuing separate identity of Scotland was guaranteed. When she died, however, Edward was accepted as the adjudicator between the twelve competitors with claims to succeed her as ruler of Scotland. He demanded that the Scottish castles, including Stirling, should be placed under his control pending his judgement and, despite misgivings on the part of some Scots, this was done in 1291. While Edward was himself staying at Stirling on 12 July 1291 arrangements were made for the Scottish nobility to swear fealty to him. On 17 November 1292, in Berwick-upon-Tweed, Edward gave judgement in favour of John Balliol, a great-great-great-grandson of David I, and he instructed that the castles were to be handed over to John. Edward evidently assumed that King John would be gratefully pliant to his wishes, but it soon became clear that, despite disagreements between the Scottish magnates, John was anxious to reestablish Scotland as an independent kingdom.

Open warfare, the first phase of what have come to be known as the Wars of Independence, eventually broke out between the two kingdoms after Edward imperiously demanded Scottish support in his wars with France in 1295. The Scots instead chose to enter into a treaty with the French against the English, the first of a long series of such treaties. In the following year Edward headed north on a punitive campaign, in the course of which he found Stirling Castle open and abandoned by the Scots except for a gate-keeper. In the ensuing years of warfare the castle was to change hands on a number of occasions. It was first retaken by the Scots after the famous victory of Andrew Murray, William Wallace and their 'army of Scotland' at the battle of Stirling Bridge in 1297, when most of the English garrison were slain along with their constable Sir Richard Waldegrave.

Before the battle, Murray and Wallace had drawn up their troops on the hill on the far side of the Forth known as Abbey Craig, where J.T. Rochead's magnificent Wallace Monument of 1859–69 now stands (5 and see colour plate 10). From the vantage point of that hill the Scots overlooked the causeway leading to the eastern end of the timber bridge over the river, which was probably a short way upstream from the present bridge. The English troops under John de Warenne, Earl of Surrey,

5 *A view from the castle across to Abbey Craig, with the bridge in the valley below.*

badly misjudged the situation. They first demanded that the Scots should submit, to which they received the resounding reply that the Scots were 'not here to make peace but to do battle to defend ourselves and liberate our kingdom'. Then, instead of attempting to out-flank the Scots by sending troops across the Forth at a higher point as one of their leaders suggested, the English forces were ordered across a bridge that was so narrow that it could accommodate columns of no more than two horsemen in width. The Scots cut this column in half and proceeded to inflict a resounding defeat upon them. In the aftermath of the battle the English leaders, William Fitz Warin, Marmaduke Tweng and William de Ros, man-aged to fight their way back to the castle, but were soon starved into surrendering it. With characteristic magnanimity Wallace spared their lives, although the flaying of the body of

Hugh Cressingham, the English treasurer of Scotland, was a less attractive gesture.

The Scots were not to enjoy the fruits of this fine victory for long. Murray died within the year, probably from wounds received in the course of the battle, and Scotland consequently lost one of its great leaders. In the following year Wallace was himself defeated at Falkirk, the last pitched battle into which the Scots were to allow themselves to be drawn for over fifteen years. In the wake of the disaster of Falkirk, Stirling had to be abandoned, and Edward I once more strengthened and provisioned the castle. The pendulum swung yet again in 1299, when Edward failed to relieve the English garri-son who were besieged by Scottish forces under Robert Bruce, Bishop William Lamberton of St Andrews and John Comyn, the Lord of Badenoch. The Scots had their base for the siege in Tor Wood, about 8km (5 miles) to the south of the castle. Edward, recognizing the importance of Stirling, had vainly urged his exhausted troops to attempt to break the siege, but ultimately had to allow his constable, John Sampson, to surrender.

Yet again, however, the Scots were to face further reverses, and by 1303 Stirling was the last major castle remaining in their hands. By this time it seemed to many of the Scottish leaders that English domination of their country was an inescapable fact, and that they had little choice but to make the best of it. Certainly Robert Bruce, Earl of Carrick, the future Robert I, had formally accepted this when he was received into Edward I's peace as early as January or February 1302, and he was with Edward in his winter quarters at Dunfermline in 1303. The continuing strategic importance of Stirling at this time is shown by the way in which Edward was forced to make elaborate provision for bypassing it, by having floating bridges made at King's Lynn in Norfolk which would allow him to cross the River Forth into Fife at a lower point. After he had reached Dunfermline, Edward began to make his preparations for the siege of Stirling, including the construction of a formidable array of at least seventeen siege engines of various kinds, suggesting he was only too well aware that the success of his future plans was dependent on the capture of the castle.

The siege began in earnest in April 1304. The Scottish garrison under Sir William Oliphant put up a courageous defence of the castle, though by that time most of the other Scottish leaders were ready to submit themselves to Edward. As a sign of the underlying loyalties of the time, however, it should be remembered that, even while the siege was in progress, Robert the Bruce and Bishop William Lamberton of St Andrews were drawing up a secret pact at Cambuskenneth Abbey, which was to pave the way for Robert's own claim to the throne of Scotland. Oliphant eventually surrendered the castle on 20 July, though in doing this he spoilt Edward's fun, because the English king had not yet had the opportunity to bring into play what was presumably a particularly ingenious siege engine known rather

ominously as 'the war wolf'. Part of the Scottish garrison was ungenerously ordered to stay within the castle while the 'wolf' was deployed, apparently with particularly devastating consequences for the gatehouse.

The death of Edward I, 'the hammer of the Scots', in 1307 must have come as a great relief to most of Scotland, particularly since it quickly became apparent that his son, Edward II, was inclined to show little of his father's singleness of purpose towards his northern neighbour. Robert Bruce, a great-great-great-great-grandson of David I, had already been enthroned and crowned as king of Scotland at Scone in 1306, and under his inspired leadership Scottish independence was progressively re-established (6). By 1313 Stirling was one of only three major castles retained by the English, the others being Berwick and Bothwell. Edward Bruce, the king's younger brother, set about besieging Stirling, which was under the

6 *The statue of Robert I on the esplanade of the castle, by A. Currie.*

21

command of Sir Philip Moubray, who was himself a Scot. With the rather quixotic chivalry that seems to have characterized so many of the Scottish actions, Edward Bruce agreed to withdraw his forces on condition that the castle would be surrendered by the English if their army failed to relieve it before midsummer's day of 1314. Robert I was highly displeased by his brother's agreement, since he was anxious to avoid pitched battles if at all possible, though his own sense of honour left him no alternative to accepting the terms that had been agreed. It was this agreement that led to the battle of Bannockburn (7, colour plate 4).

Edward II was for once resolute in his determination to suppress firmly what he regarded as a 'wicked rebellion of Robert Bruce and his accomplices in the king's [that is, the English king's] land of Scotland', and there was nothing half-hearted about his preparations to relieve Stirling. By the same token, for Robert I it was equally essential that the English were not allowed to retain control of any part of his kingdom. With such determination on both sides, when battle was finally joined on 23 June, about 4km (2½ miles) south of the castle, the outcome was far from certain. After a rendezvous at Tor Wood, Robert's forces had moved on to shelter in the nearby New Park that had been enclosed by Alexander III in 1263, and it seems he may even have had thoughts of withdrawing from there. The first day of the battle involved a number of individually inconclusive encounters. Yet a display of great personal prowess by the king himself, when he killed Sir Henry de Bohun in single combat, along with indications that the tightly packed schiltrons of Scottish foot-soldiers (roughly circular formations with spearmen holding spears outwards around the perimeter) could be a match for the English cavalry, did

7 A fifteenth-century depiction of the battle of Bannockburn, with Stirling Castle in the background (by permission, Master and Fellows of Corpus Christi College Cambridge, MS 171, f.265r.).

much to boost Scottish morale. Despite this, the Scots continued to feel wary of pitched battles with the numerically superior English, and may have still considered withdrawing before a second day's fighting could take place. This changed when it was heard from Sir Alexander Seton – a Scot who had been fighting with the English – that the English had been greatly disheartened by the fighting so far.

After the cease of hostilities on that first day, during the evening of 23 June the English troops regrouped themselves in a triangular marshy area defined on one side by the Forth and on another by the Bannock burn. They must presumably have thought they would have the opportunity to form themselves into a more effective array before battle was rejoined. However, as soon as dawn broke on the following day, three of the Scottish battalions descended on them in force, giving the English little chance to regroup in the face of the inexorable onslaught, and Robert's own battalion followed to drive home the victory. The defeated English king tried to take refuge in the castle, but was thwarted in this when Moubray said he intended to surrender the castle in keeping with the agreement of 1313. Edward thus had no alternative to making his way back to England as best he could, by way of Dunbar. Following his honourable surrender of the castle, Sir Philip Moubray was allowed to change allegiance and join his Scottish compatriots.

As a result of Robert I's impressive leadership, the battle of Bannockburn was a triumph for the Scots that has been rightly characterized as the most important of the few truly decisive battles to be fought on Scottish soil. But, despite such a highly prestigious victory in a pitched battle, and the consequent firmer establishment of his authority within Scotland, Robert I still felt that his greatest strength against the risk of further attack lay in mobility, and orders were given to destroy the defences of Stirling Castle so that it could not be held against him again. This was a policy followed at several other castles.

23

Stirling Castle and the second phase of the wars with England

Tragically, the peace that was ushered in by the victory of Bannockburn was of only relatively short duration. Robert I died in 1329, and was succeeded by his son, David II, who was then a child of only five years old. By that time the English throne was occupied by Edward III, who was prepared to take almost as close an interest in Scottish affairs as had his grandfather. In 1332 Edward Balliol, son of the King John who had been nominated by Edward I in 1292, took advantage of the new king's minority to invade Scotland. In doing this he had the support of Edward III himself, and also that of those Scots who had lost their estates as a consequence of their English allegiance, and who were thus known as the 'disinherited'. Much of Scotland progressively capitulated before this latest onslaught, and by 1333 it was necessary for the young David II to be taken to France for his own safety. He returned to his kingdom in 1341, but five years later, during a sortie into England, he was captured at the battle of Neville's Cross and remained in English captivity until he was thirty-three, in 1357.

Stirling Castle was under English control from at least 1336, when Sir Thomas Rokeby is known to have been its warden. Andrew Murray (son of the Andrew Murray who had been the comrade-in-arms of Wallace), who was reappointed guardian of the kingdom for the Scots in that year, attempted to take the castle back from the English by siege in 1337. During this campaign guns may have been used, perhaps for only the third time that they had been deployed on Scottish soil. In the event Murray was forced to withdraw, but there was a second siege by Robert the Steward (the future Robert II) in 1341–2. It was at this time that David II was briefly back in his kingdom, between his return from France and his capture at Neville's Cross. Having their king within his kingdom may have reinforced the Scottish resolve, and the English garrison was starved into surrender. Although there was to be a further English onslaught on the kingdom in 1347, while David II was in English captivity, Stirling, together with Edinburgh and Dunbar, remained under Scottish control.

Sir Thomas Rokeby and the English had clearly believed they were in Scotland to stay in 1336, and there are records of a considerable amount of work within Stirling Castle. Accounts for 1336–7 refer to various buildings with walls of timber and mud, and roofing of turves. These included accommodation that was presumably of high quality, such as a hall and chambers, and also more mundane offices such as a kitchen, brewhouse and larders. This reminds us that there was no inconsistency in the way that even important buildings might still be erected of such relatively impermant materials, and of course their finished appearance when plastered and painted was probably very little different from that of masonry structures. Even an enclosure referred to as a 'peel' on the north side of the inner bailey was being constructed of timber daubed with mortar, with a projecting wall-head fighting gallery known as a bretasche. However, by this time the main defences of the castle seem to have been increasingly at least partly of stone, and there are references to masonry work on walls and turrets, as well as to the construction of a drawbridge. The high wall between the inner and outer baileys was apparently 46m (150ft) long.

It must be said that, during all of this time, we have very little idea of how the buildings and fortifications of the castle would have looked, though from this point onwards there is an increase in the records of building activity at the castle. These records are particularly fascinating for showing how much work was constantly needed at a major royal castle.

Stirling Castle under the earlier Stewarts

David II died in 1371, and was succeeded by the first of the Stewart kings, the ageing

Robert II, who was a grandson of Robert I by his daughter Marjory Bruce (**8**). Robert progressively transferred much of his power to his eldest son, John Earl of Carrick (who eventually succeeded him to the throne in 1390 as Robert III), though, following a kick by a horse in 1388, Carrick himself became a permanent invalid. Much of the real power of the monarchy was then transferred to another of Robert's sons, Robert Earl of Menteith and Fife, who eventually became Duke of Albany in 1398. Albany's role in the death of one of his nephews in 1402 and in the capture of the other (the future James I) by the English in 1406 may have been innocent, but the subsequent death of his heart-broken brother, Robert III, that year was to leave Albany himself in effective control of the kingdom until his own death in 1420.

From at least the early 1380s Albany's greatest architectural interests were probably centred on his own castle of Doune, 9.6km (*c.* 6 miles) north-west of Stirling. But during the reigns of Albany's father and brother, and throughout his own governorship, the Exchequer Rolls record much construction work at Stirling, and Albany must have been an instigator of some of this. Apart from anything else, it would have been an essential demonstration of his own vice-regal powers to be both resident and architecturally active at the principal royal castles, and it was at Stirling that he died.

Much of the building activity of the later fourteenth century and earlier fifteenth appears to have centred on the defences along the main lines of approach to the castle. In 1380 and 1381 there are references to a forework and a barbican, while in 1404 a drawbridge again figures in the records. It is tempting to suspect that these could have been on the line of the forework we now see (see **31**), which was built a century later, and certainly there are traces of earlier work beneath its western end. Also referred to in 1381 is a north gate, and this reminds us that there was almost certainly a

8 *An engraving of the great seal of Robert II.*

second entrance to the castle at this time, from the valley between the castle rock and Gowan Hill. The north gate, which still serves as the way from the main enclosure of the castle to the nether bailey, is a structure that has been altered on many occasions, but there are good reasons for thinking that the basis of what we now see is what was under construction in 1381 (**9** and see **26**). The upper parts of this gatehouse are traditionally referred to as the mint; however, although we know that coins were minted at Stirling, the balance of probability is in favour of this process having been carried out within the burgh rather than at the castle. Other accounts of the period relate to structures inside the defences. The building of a prison and the repair of some houses is referred to in 1402, and the construction of two chambers in 1415, while in 1412 the chapel of St Michael was rebuilt. So far as the last of these is concerned, it is possible that this chapel could be represented by one of the sets of foundations known to run diagonally beneath its successor of 1594 (see **13**). Walls of at least two earlier buildings have been found below the present chapel, the earlier of which was a relatively small rectangular building.

From all of this we see how the wide range of functions that had to be accommodated within a major castle was being met by operations paid for from the royal exchequer, and it may yet prove possible to identify the remains of them in existing buildings, or in some of the foundations that are occasionally found through excavation. The eccentrically aligned building between the

9 *The outer face of the north gate, with the great hall rising behind the north curtain-wall.*

palace and the King's Old Building at the south-west corner of the inner close, for example, might conceivably incorporate the remains of earlier work than on first sight seems likely (**10**). Could it have housed the two chambers mentioned in 1415? The later royal accommodation was placed to either side of this block, possibly because the buildings set aside for royal occupation had always been sited on the highest point of the castle rock, and this could certainly point to some relatively prestigious original use for this block (see **2**).

Following the return of James I from English captivity in March 1424 we begin to hear ever more about the castle. It appears to have been granted to his queen, Joan Beaufort, as part of her jointure (the property settled on her at her marriage), and this was also to be the case with the marriage settlements of a number of later queens. Soon after he had become settled in his kingdom it became clear that James was less than content with the efforts that had been made by his kinsmen in attempting to negotiate his release. Duke Robert of Albany was by that time dead and out of reach, but his son, Duke Murdoch, had succeeded him as governor, and James decided to move against him and his family. The process began at the parliament of 1425 in Perth, and they were tried before a further session of parliament held on 24 May that year in Stirling. As a result, Murdoch and two of his sons were beheaded in front of Stirling Castle.

James's own increasingly high-handed actions were eventually to make him a number of dangerous enemies, and he was to be murdered in the Dominican friary at Perth in 1437. Soon after this, in an attempt to keep control over her son, Queen Joan is said to have smuggled the six-year-old James II from Edinburgh into her castle of Stirling by carrying him in a chest. This is perhaps unlikely, though it was certainly at Stirling two years later that she suffered indignities at the hands of the Livingstone family, following her second marriage to Sir James Stewart. After she had herself been imprisoned within the castle by Sir Alexander Livingstone, she eventually had to agree to grant him the use of the castle as the place for the upbringing of the royal children. Royal minorities could be difficult times for dowager queens!

James I's harsh treatment of some of the magnates, particularly those who were members of his own family, had left a void in the ranks of the nobility that allowed other families to rise to greater power. Among those families were the already powerful earls of Douglas, who took the precaution of building up alliances aimed at mutual assistance. Such alliances were naturally felt to be contrary to the royal interest, and in an attempt to solve this problem through diplomatic discussion, the eighth Earl of Douglas was invited to Stirling Castle on 21 February 1452, under the promise of James II's special protection. Unfortunately, when the earl proved obdurate the following day, the headstrong king 'stert sodanly till him with ane knyf and strak him in the collar and doun the bodie', while one courtier struck out his brains with a pole-axe and a number of others made their own bloody contributions to the earl's end. Traditionally this is said to have happened in a room at the northern end of the King's Old Building, though this is impossible since that building cannot have existed as we now see it by 1452 (see **17**). It is perhaps more likely that it took place in an earlier chamber of the king's lodging, which could be a chamber that had been referred to in the accounts for 1434.

Three years earlier in the reign of James II, Stirling had been the backdrop for a remarkable tournament. This was in 1449, the year of the king's marriage to Mary, a daughter of the Duke of Guelders in the Low Countries, and a niece of the Duke of Burgundy. At this tournament two Burgundian knights, Simon and Jacques de Lalain, with their squire Meriadet, were pitched against two members of the Douglas family and John Ross of Halket. The Burgundians were probably the victors by a narrow margin. Martial sports of this type were one way of practising for warfare in earnest, and also helped to direct the aggression of the magnates into acceptable channels. Such formalized chivalry, with its emphasis on honour, was also an important element in the ambience of late medieval and Renaissance kingship and, as we shall see, may eventually have been reflected in some aspects of the

10 *The building at the south end of the King's Old Building.*

architecture produced at Stirling as the setting for the Scottish court.

Relatively little building, however, is recorded for the reign of James II at Stirling, though this is likely to be partly because of the scantness of the surviving accounts at this period. We do know from what he built at Ravenscraig Castle in Fife, and from the efforts that he made to build up a royal arsenal, that James was deeply interested in the problems of how castles should respond to the growing threat of artillery. One intriguing possibility is suggested by a schematic representation of Stirling Castle that appears in the background of a depiction of the battle of Bannockburn, in a copy of the *Scotichronicon* of around the 1440s now at Corpus Christi College, Cambridge (see **7**). This shows one of the towers with shot-holes suitable for artillery and, since such shot-holes seem to have first appeared in Scotland during the reign of James II, this could indicate that the artist was showing something of the most recent works at the castle. Unfortunately, James's interest in artillery was to be – quite literally – the death of him, when he stood too close to a cannon that burst at the siege of Roxburgh in 1460.

James III

Tradition has attributed a considerable amount of building in Stirling Castle to James III (**11**). In his *Historie*, written in the later sixteenth century, Robert Lindsay of Pitscottie said that James considered Stirling his most pleasant residence, and that he founded the Chapel Royal and built the great hall within it. Bearing in mind that Lindsay can be rather unreliable as a historian, recent writers have tended to doubt that so much building can be attributed to the third James. It is certainly true that both the architectural evidence and the surviving

accounts make it almost certain that the hall we now see is later than his reign. We also know that the Chapel Royal was not in fact formally instituted as a college until after his death; indeed, so far as we know, James's main efforts to establish Chapels Royal were at Restalrig, on the outskirts of Edinburgh, and at Coldingham Priory on the Berwickshire coast.

In James III's favour as a significant patron of architecture, however, it should be remembered

11 *James III, from the altarpiece painted by Hugo van der Goes for Trinity College Chapel in Edinburgh, and now displayed in the National Galleries of Scotland (The Royal Collection © 1994 Her Majesty Queen Elizabeth II).*

that he occupied the throne over a relatively long period, between the accidental death of his father in 1460 and his own murder in 1488. In addition, he is said to have taken more pleasure in the company of craftsmen than of his magnates, though it is doubtful if the largely apocryphal figure of Thomas Cochrane really was responsible for the design of some of his buildings as used to be believed. It must also be said in James's favour that those limited records which happen to have survived do show that he was an active builder at the castle. There are references to building of a 'white tower' in 1463, and to works on the castle walls in 1467. There are also accounts for extensive works on the chapel roof between 1467 and 1469, for which Thomas Bully was apparently one master of the fabric. Whether these represented the final stages of raising a new building, or a refurbishing of the chapel of St Michael referred to in 1412, we simply cannot know.

Beyond all of this, around this period we begin to build up a picture of the pleasant amenities that were available to the king at Stirling. We hear, for example, of extensive gardening works at various dates, and it seems that deer were being brought up from Ettrick for hunting in the park in 1461. On a more martial note, James Nory was making artillery in a gun-house at the castle in 1475, and it would be particularly interesting to know where that was taking place. The only possible clue is that excavations below the chapel in 1994 found what looked like the waste from a foundry in the spoil that was thrown into the demolished foundations of its predecessor on the site. It must be admitted, however, that this waste could have resulted from one of a number of industrial processes.

Taking account of all of this, it is irrefutable that James III was responsible for not insignificant building operations at Stirling Castle, and for enhancing it as a setting for his court. It is possible that the chapel he either rebuilt or refurbished is at least partly represented by the second set of foundations that have been found on the north side of the upper square, where they are largely covered by the later Chapel Royal of 1594 (12, 13, 14). Although we cannot be certain of the use of the building to which those foundations belonged, there are grounds for thinking that, wherever possible, there was continuity of use of a chapel site, even when the building itself was repeatedly reconstructed, so it is attractive to think that the present chapel may overlie earlier ones. A number of factors support the idea of these foundations belonging to a chapel. A relatively long-term ecclesiastical use for the building is suggested by the finding of a carved bishop's head of around the earlier sixteenth century at their east end in 1986 (see 30). Some further incidental support can be drawn from the fact that they are aligned relatively accurately from east to west, as was preferred for medieval churches and chapels; though, since several other buildings in the castle are on this same alignment, this does not constitute proof. Nevertheless, we do know from a report on the poor state of the castle in 1583 that the chapel was in the inner close and, since the other sides of the close were by then occupied, it could hardly have been in any other position.

Partial reinvestigation of these foundations in 1993 and 1994 has shown that they rise from the sloping bedrock that underlies this part of the castle. Although in places they have been found to rise to a height of over 3m (10ft) above the irregular rock surface, their generally rough facing, with one exception, shows that they belonged to substructures rather than to the main body of any building. At least two periods of buildings are represented by what has been found. Three walls may represent parts of the east, south and west walls of an earlier rectangular building and, as already suggested, it is tempting to suspect these could have been relics of the chapel of St Michael rebuilt in 1412, or of an even older building. The later structure also seems to have been basically rectangular, but with some evidence for narrower sections

12 *The excavated wall of an earlier building below the Chapel Royal.*

along at least part of each side, which could have been aisles. If this building was indeed the chapel, a projection on the south side might represent a porch, and there may have been a larger offshoot towards the eastern end of the north flank, in which position it was perhaps a sacristy. There was possibly an undercroft below the eastern end of the main space, where the natural rock surface shelves steeply downwards, and the inner faces of this were the only ones brought to any degree of finish.

From its scale and complexity this was clearly a very grand building in its final state. If it was indeed a chapel, it might be thought that it would have been designed to house the collegiate Chapel Royal which, as already said, is known to have been founded by James III's son, James IV. However, since it will be seen below that a chapel in this position would have blocked the entrance to the great hall, which is known to have been built to its present form by James IV, it seems most unlikely that these foundations could belong to any chapel set out by him. On balance it thus seems more reasonable to assume that the foundations represent the chapel on which James III is known to have worked rather than anything built later by James IV.

As already briefly mentioned above, a number of other buildings were set out on a parallel alignment to these foundations (see **13**). The most complete of these is on the opposite side of the inner close, at the southern end of the King's Old Building, and this block has already been tentatively referred to above in connection with the possibility that it could have contained the chambers that appear in the accounts for 1415

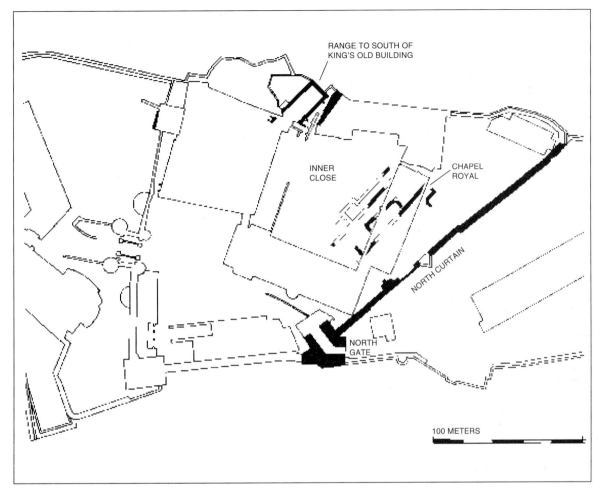

RANGE TO SOUTH OF
KING'S OLD BUILDING

INNER
CLOSE

CHAPEL
ROYAL

NORTH CURTAIN

NORTH
GATE

100 METERS

13 *A plan of the castle showing the diagonally aligned walls that either still exist or that have been found through excavation (cf. fig. 15).*

14 *Excavation and recording of the diagonally aligned foundations located below the southeastern corner of the Chapel Royal in 1994.*

(see **10**). The south wall of the King's Old Building itself may also reflect this alignment, and further parallel foundations have been found under the north-west angle of the palace. It is possible that such a disposition of buildings was encouraged by the orientation of the chapel along the north side of the close, and by that of the curtain wall between the main enclosure of the castle and the nether bailey beyond it, together with the north gate which interconnected the two parts. Although this wall is

largely sixteenth century in its present form, it is likely to follow the line of its predecessor (see 9). All of this suggests that, before the very end of the fifteenth century, the buildings on the summit of the castle rock were set out to a rather different pattern from that we now see.

Whatever his architectural contributions to Stirling, however, James III was on no assessment an attractive character, and it is hard not to conclude that many of the difficulties that overshadowed his later years were the product of his own deviousness. Some of those difficulties were centred on the castle. This was partly because his queen, Margaret of Denmark, spent the last three years of her own life within its walls before her death in 1486, possibly in order to ensure the safety of the heir to the throne, James Duke of Rothesay. Many writers have suggested that the relationship between the royal couple was almost impossibly strained during the queen's last years, and it is true that she had consented to see the king's rebellious brother, Alexander Duke of Albany, within the castle in 1482. This was probably something that the deeply suspicious king would never have been able to forget. Despite this, it is known that the king visited her at Stirling not long before her death, which may indicate that the royal couple were not so totally estranged as some have suggested.

Stirling eventually played a part in the king's death, because it was from there that the fourteen-year-old Duke of Rothesay went to join the magnates who had risen against his father on 2 February 1488, and thus provided them with the figurehead that greatly increased their chances of success. After a frantic attempt to consolidate his support, James III was eventually killed on 11 June following the battle that has come to be known as Sauchieburn, and which was fought in an area very close to the site of the battle of Bannockburn. He is said to have fallen from his horse in attempting to leap across the Bannock burn, when in unescorted flight from the field of battle; having been taken to a nearby mill to recover, he was murdered by an enemy soldier masquerading as a priest. His body was taken for burial to Cambuskenneth Abbey, where his queen already lay, and the two of them are now commemorated by a tomb constructed on the orders of Queen Victoria in 1865. The new king, James IV, evidently felt real remorse for his part in his father's death, and Robert Lindsay of Pitscottie says that it was to the head of the chapel at Stirling that he shortly afterwards made his confession. His self-inflicted penance was to wear an iron belt, which he annually increased in weight.

CHAPTER TWO

The setting for kingship

James IV: the Renaissance monarch

James IV (1488–1513) did more than any other king to make Stirling Castle the magnificent architectural setting for a royal court of European standing that we now see. Indeed, it is not too much to say that his reign marks a new epoch in the history of the castle since, for the first time, we can begin to relate upstanding architectural remains of the highest calibre with the surviving documentation of the building operations (**15, 16**).

It hardly needs stating that the production of fine architecture requires a sympathetic climate of thought and, building on foundations that may have been laid by his father, James IV

did much to foster such a climate. This is perhaps most obvious in the way that, in the course of his reign, Scotland became increasingly receptive to the Classically inspired humanist thinking that was spreading across Europe from Renaissance Italy. His own early education may well have been imbued with many of these ideas, and among those likely to have contributed was the fine scholar Archibald Whitelaw, who had been James III's own tutor and who was now the royal secretary. His mother, Margaret of Denmark, who was a highly intelligent woman, probably

15 *A plan of the castle in its present state (Sylvia Stevenson).*

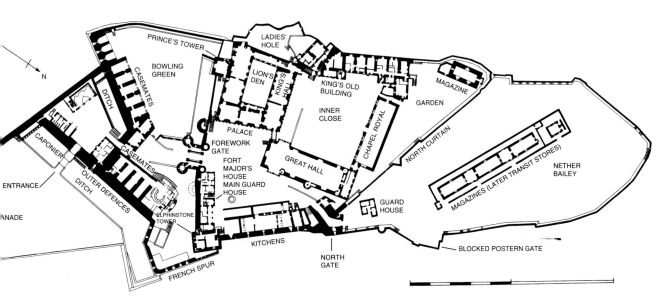

16 *James IV (by permission, Scottish National Portrait Gallery).*

played a significant role in the planning of the young prince's education in her years at Stirling. As one pointer to the intellectual climate of the times, it should be remembered that it was to be during James IV's reign that such poets as Gavin Douglas composed verse which showed a more profound knowledge of Classical antiquity than anything heard previously from Scottish writers.

A different aspect of the search for new knowledge is seen in the way that the Italian John Damian was accommodated in Stirling Castle, while he carried out his alchemical experiments to find the fifth essence that would change ordinary metals into gold. To fund this expensive research, money was granted to him from the revenues of the Premonstratensian abbey of Tongland in Kirkcudbrightshire. Damian is now best remembered for the way in which, at a time when his hold over the king was perhaps

weakening and dramatic measures were called for, he attempted a flight to France from the walls of Stirling Castle in September 1507. As might have been expected with wings of his own making, Damian's flight was less than a total success, and apparently ended in a midden below the castle walls. He is said to have concluded ruefully that he had made a mistake in using hens' feathers, since they had a more natural affinity for the midden than for the skies. In retrospect, Damian's exploits seem absurd, though we must remember that much of what we know of him comes from William Dunbar who, despite his own great merits as a poet, was not above envying those whom he thought were receiving greater royal favour than himself. It must be assumed that Damian's scientific experiments were regarded more seriously by many of his contemporaries, including the king himself.

One of our sources of information on the king is a letter written in 1498 by the Spanish ambassador, Don Pedro de Ayala, when James was still a relatively young man. Such accounts must always be treated with caution since there might be some underlying motive for their composition, but there is much that sounds convincing in this case. James was apparently a highly accomplished linguist, with particular abilities in Latin; he was also said to be pious, and though piety was expected of kings it was evidently true enough. Especially convincing is Ayala's suggestion that James's natural high courage could lead to impetuous behaviour. This last characteristic is emphasized in a less flattering description sent to the English court by Sir John Ramsay, and may have been ultimately one reason for the catastrophe of Flodden in 1513.

James's personal courage was also evident in his love of tournaments, in which he was fond of taking part personally. Beyond the political message of such tournaments, there was at least an element of romanticism, as is particularly evident from the 'counterfuting of the round tabill of King Arthour' which was a central feature of the

Edinburgh tournament of 1508. There was in fact a much greater interest in the Arthurian legend in Scotland than is often appreciated, and references to Arthur as a conqueror of Scotland are frequent in Bower's *Scotichronicon*. The fifteenth-century writer William of Worcester suggested that Stirling was itself the home of the Order of the Knights of the Round Table. Some later historians even suggested that the seventeenth-century earthworks of the royal gardens below the castle walls were the actual setting for the round table, while one modern writer, Norma Lorre Goodrich, has argued that Stirling was Camelot. Be that as it may, this interest in a chivalric past in the time of James IV could have been one factor behind the design of some of the buildings raised for him at Stirling, which are in some ways almost self-consciously medieval in spirit.

Stirling was to be the setting for much of wider importance that took place in James's reign. It was there that in 1495 he received Perkin Warbeck, the highly dubious claimant to the English throne, through his claims to be variously a bastard son of Richard III, the Earl of Warwick or the Duke of York. It is not clear how far James believed his claims, though his reception in Scotland was doubtlessly a splendid opportunity to cock a snook at his future father-in-law, Henry VII of England. On a more personal level, in 1496 James chose to ensconce his mistress, Margaret Drummond, in the castle, though she was later transferred to Linlithgow.

To provide a suitable setting for his monarchy, James IV pushed forward a programme of palace building in all the principal royal residences of his kingdom on a scale that was quite unprecedented in Scotland. In doing this one motive was doubtlessly a wish to show himself as the equal of his contemporaries, Louis XII of France and Henry VII of England. Major operations at Edinburgh, Falkland, Holyrood and Linlithgow resulted in a series of magnificent buildings of a scale and quality that certainly surpassed anything previously achieved in Scotland; though in several cases we know that

his father, grandfather and great-grandfather had already made a start in providing fine residences at those places. But it is at Stirling that James's architectural aspirations can now be seen both at their grandest, and in a state that is least modified either by later rebuilding or by excessively creative modern restoration.

In most of James's palatial enterprises the buildings are set out around the sides of a more or less rectangular open area. At Stirling, as also at his other favourite castle of Edinburgh, the chief royal enclave was a courtyard on the summit of the rock. This is sometimes now referred to as the upper square, but was earlier known as the inner close. It was probably James who took the first steps towards forming this courtyard by moving away from the earlier diagonal alignment of buildings that has been discussed above (see **13**).

James IV's lodging

Among James's many works on the castle was evidently the construction of a new self-contained residential range for himself in the 1490s. By this stage of the royal accounting processes most of the detailed references to building operations are in the accounts of the Lord High Treasurer rather than in the Exchequer Rolls. Those treasurer's accounts refer to a contract with the master mason Walter Merlioun for what was described as the King's House in June 1496, though this contract may have been simply a formality, because the accounts also show that the house was nearing completion within that same year. Merlioun was a member of a prominent family of master masons who were frequently employed in the royal service. Walter himself was involved in other building operations for the king at Dunbar Castle and Holyrood Palace, as well as being at work on the great burgh church of Perth in the same year that he was building the king's residence at Stirling.

In recent years a great deal of structural work has been carried out on the range that

17 *The King's Old Building.*

runs along the west side of the inner close, both to stabilize a building that is perilously close to the edge of a precipice, and to make it suitable for use as a regimental museum for the Argyll and Sutherland Highlanders (**17**). This building has been known as the King's Old Work since at least 1687, and more recently as the King's Old Building. As a result of the findings made during work on it in the 1970s and 1980s, it is now thought highly likely that it is this building that is identifiable with the royal residence of 1496. The identification is both on account of its planning, which is what might be expected in a royal lodging of the period, and because of the similarity of the moulded stone details of its doorways and windows with those of the great hall on the opposite side of the close, which is also the

work of James IV. Such mouldings are often one of the surest ways of testing the relationship between buildings.

It must be said that the King's Old Building has been extensively altered on many occasions, and that in consequence it is now only barely recognizable for what it may once have been. Nevertheless, it is evident that it originally had two large principal rooms on the first floor, which were carried on an undercroft of five vaulted rooms at ground-floor level, each of those ground-floor rooms having a window and doorway looking on to the inner close (**18**). The principal rooms were reached by a wide spiral stair in a square tower-like projection, and increased prominence was given to this stair by capping it with an octagonal superstructure. The planning of these rooms would certainly be consistent with their use as the main rooms of a royal lodging, which at this period would probably have consisted of a hall followed by one or more chambers. The hall was the more public room, and was reached directly from the stair, though there is likely to have been a screened-off vestibule at the entrance end. The chamber beyond it could serve as both an imposing bedroom and as a more private living-room for the king. From survey drawings of the castle made in 1719 and 1741, it seems the main rooms probably rose up into the roof space, where they were covered by a tunnel-like ceiling of polygonal cross-section. Fragments of dark green glazed floor-tiles have been found within the window embrasures, and these, possibly combined with other tiles to form a suitable pattern, would have covered the whole floor.

Beyond the royal chamber it might be expected that there would have been a small number of more intimately scaled chambers or closets. In the King's Old Building there was indeed a lower range at right angles to the north end of the main block, leading off what is assumed to have been the royal chamber, and this probably contained such closets. It is tempting to suspect it was these which were

18 *A sketch-plan of the ground and first floors of the King's Old Building showing the likely original arrangement (Sylvia Stevenson).*

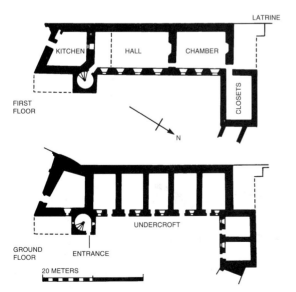

referred to as *cors chalmeris* (cross-chambers) in the accounts. In the angle between the main block and the wing there is known to have been a second spiral stair and, though this seems not to have been an original feature, it could have been added at some stage to provide a more private means of access to the chamber and closets. A short way behind this cross-range, and set into the main curtain-wall of the castle where it could drain over the rock face, was a latrine turret. At the opposite, the southern, end of the lodging was a room of irregular plan, and from the size of its fireplace it perhaps served as a kitchen for the royal lodging. Its irregular plan was because it seems to have made use of existing walls, the end one being on a similar alignment as a pair of chambers beyond it, which have already been referred to above as probably being of earlier date (see **10**).

There is a great deal that we do not understand about this building, though some of the mysteries might be explained if there once had been timber galleries at the northern end of the chamber and in front of the kitchen block (**19**). Such timber galleries were certainly far more common than is often now appreciated. Nevertheless, we know enough to understand that it could have provided an extremely imposing lodging for the king, on what must always have been the most elevated and prestigious part of the castle, where it could enjoy spectacular views across Flanders Moss to the hills around Loch Lomond (see **3**). What provision there would have been for lodging a queen at this date is not known, though the king was still a bachelor in 1496, only marrying Margaret Tudor seven years later in 1503.

Fine architecture designed for royal use was always a potential source of ideas for the buildings of the king's greater subjects, and it is interesting to see how the King's Old Building was an inspiration for a range constructed at Castle Campbell, a few kilometres to the east of Stirling. Castle Campbell was the principal Lowland residence of the earls of

19 *A conjectural sketch of the original appearance of the King's Old Building (David Pollock).*

20 *The hall range at Castle Campbell.*

Argyll, and on the south side of its courtyard there is a range which bears a striking resemblance to the King's Old Building, especially in the octagonal superstructure of the stair tower which gave access to its main floor (20). The earls of Argyll were prominent courtiers, the first earl being chancellor of the kingdom; however, he died in 1493, and so it seems likely to have been the second earl, who died with his king at Flodden, who was the instigator of the Castle Campbell range.

The great hall and associated buildings

Writing in the later sixteenth century, Lindsay of Pitscottie stated that the great hall had been built by James III's supposed favourite, Thomas Cochrane. But from the surviving documents there can be little doubt that it was largely, or even completely, the work of James IV. The treasurer's accounts record work on a building known as the old hall in the early years of the sixteenth century and, though we do not know where this was, it does suggest by implication that the new hall had been started by then. That new hall must itself have been already nearing completion by 1503, because a plasterer was then at work on its walls. An interesting aspect of this reference to plastering is that the craftsman involved was specified as being English at a time when relationships with England were rather less strained than they had been for many years. The renewed contact with English ideas may also be evident in the overall design of the great hall at Stirling.

The hall was set out on a large scale, with overall dimensions of about 42 by 14.25m (138 by 47ft) , which compares very favourably with those of the hall at Edinburgh Castle, of only about 29 by 12.5m (95 by 41ft) (21). On account of the steep slope of the land towards the east, it was carried on a massive barrel-vaulted substructure not dissimilar from that of the King's Old Building. (Vaulted substructures were also necessary for the hall at Edinburgh Castle, though there they were not so closely

21 *The south gable of the great hall in course of restoration.*

tied to the plan of the hall.) As originally built, this substructure probably raised the floor of the hall itself slightly above the level of the bottom end of the inner close, though later changes to the external levels mean that the bottom of the close is now approximately at the same height as the hall floor. Initially the hall was separated from the close by a sunken transe-like area; since doorways and windows open from the substructure into this transe, it was probably crossed by no more than a bridge to the main entrance of the hall. Running along the close side of the hall, at about half its height, was a lean-to roof which was probably carried on a line of timber posts. This roof would thus have protected both the sunken transe and the entrance to the hall. However, the transe was later covered by a stone vault and the ground surface of the square was extended over this.

The main entrance into the hall was by a doorway towards the northern end of the main

22 *The castle from the east by John Slezer, showing the mid-sixteenth-century artillery spur, with the forework and great hall behind* (Theatrum Scotiae, 1693).

façade and, as might be expected, it originally opened into a vestibule within the hall, separated from the main space by a screen and with a loft above it. Later, after the palace had been built adjacent to the south-west corner of the hall, there was also a royal entrance directly on to the dais at the southern end of the hall. Particular emphasis was always given to that dais by two vast bay windows, one set on each side, and these windows must have flooded the south end of the hall with light (see **24**). The main lighting for the rest of the hall was through pairs of rectangular windows in the side and end walls, set about 5m (16½ft) above floor level (see **89**). Rather unusually, the glazing was on the inner plane of the wall, and the windows were externally framed by outward-splaying embrasures with segmentally arched heads. Internally, the walls below the windows were presumably originally covered with hangings of some kind.

Five fireplaces were required to heat such a

vast space: one behind the dais would have kept the king comfortably warm, while the rest of the hall was heated by two fireplaces in each of the side walls. There were four spiral stairways at various points in the hall. Of the two within the screened-off vestibule, one simply ran from the main floor down to the basement, while the other ran the full height of the building, from basement to wall-head, opening on to both the main level and the platform above the vestibule. A third stair, near the mid-point of the east wall, similarly ran much of the full height of the building, but it also opened into a trumpeters' loft within the wall thickness at the level of the high windows. A fourth stair, on the north side of the dais, ran from the hall to a mezzanine level of the basement, though this stair may have been suppressed at a relatively early stage in its existence since it is shown in none of the seventeenth- or eighteenth-century plans of the hall and castle.

Slezer's views of the castle, published in the 1690s, show that, as is to be expected in a royal building of the early sixteenth century, the hall had a crenellated (embattled) parapet around the walkway at the wall-head (see **22**).

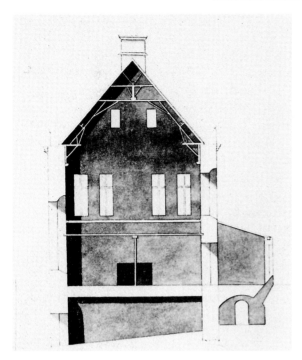

23 *The section through the great hall from the survey of 1719, showing the form of the hammerbeam roof (Crown copyright, National Library of Scotland, B.O. Z2/18b).*

This seems to have been carried around the cap-houses of those stairways which rose to the wall-head to create what are sometimes known as *chemins-de-ronde*. Set behind the parapet was the roof, which was contained by gables above the two end walls. This roof was a magnificent structure of hammerbeam construction, very similar to, but not quite identical with, that over the hall in Edinburgh Castle. The roof was still in place in 1789–91 according to Francis Grose, but seems to have been removed shortly before 1800 when the hall was subdivided to form a barrack block. Our main evidence for its form is two measured drawings which formed part of surveys of the castle prepared in 1719 and 1741 (23). The hall is an invaluable indicator of architectural tastes within Scotland in the years around 1500. In the roughly contemporary hall at Edinburgh Castle a small number of precociously Classical details show the very early beginnings of the influence of such architectural ideas in Renaissance Scotland. But the hall at Stirling is still almost defiantly a building in the medieval tradition, in both its layout and its detailing. The strongly longitudinal plan, with high bay windows at one end, probably reflects the influence of the English late medieval approach to the design of major halls. More specifically, it could have been a building such as the hall that had been built by Edward IV at Eltham in Kent in the later 1470s that was the particular source of inspiration. It is perhaps worth noting here that James may also have planned a similar hall with a dais flanked by bay windows for the north side of the courtyard of his palace at Falkland in Fife, though that would have been on a much smaller scale. The most strikingly English feature of the hall at Stirling must have been the hammerbeam roof, since such roofs were one of the particular glories of a number of royal halls south of the border, as at Westminster and Eltham, and later at Hampton Court.

Other essentially medieval features of the design were the surface application of ribs to the arches of the bay windows (which made them look like ribbed vaults) (24), the elaborately enriched image-niches along the two long

24 *The west bay of the great hall.*

façades (25) and, on a smaller scale, the niches running up the bay window on the east face. This bay window also has the delightful feature of a band of intersecting arches as the horizontal transoms at the mid-height of the individual lights. The crenellated parapet at the wall-head was a further essentially medieval feature, though this had come to be regarded as an almost indispensable feature of a high-status building of the period, and no longer had more than nominal defensive connotations. However, if this parapet was indeed carried around the stair cap-houses as *chemins-de-ronde*, as seems to be suggested by Slezer, this is as likely to have been an idea of ultimately French as of English origin. The intersecting arcs of the transoms in the east bay could also owe something to continental prototypes. From all of this we can readily appreciate how the assimilation of architectural ideas was a highly complex matter at this period, and there was no sense of inconsistency in drawing ideas from the wide range of sources with which Scotland enjoyed contact.

The hall was intended to provide an impressive space which could fittingly house great occasions in the life of the court and State, in a way that would demonstrate to all who saw it the power and standing of Scotland's monarchs (see 53). It was certainly not an everyday 'living-room' in the way that the great hall of an earlier castle might have been. Nevertheless, eating was an essential part of the hospitality associated with such great occasions, and this meant that kitchens were required in the close vicinity of the hall.

25 *An angel corbel from one of the tabernacles on the west face of the great hall.*

26 *The inner face of the north gate.*

27 *The first-floor rooms within the north gate before recent conservation, which were remodelled for use as kitchens to serve the great hall.*

The earliest of those kitchens seems to have been constructed on the upper floor of the north gateway which connected the main enclosure of the castle and the nether bailey (**26**). As has been suggested above, this gate was almost certainly part of the work that was carried out for Robert II in 1381, though it had been enlarged since then. There are accounts for work on a kitchen tower by a mason named as John in 1503, although this may refer to part of the forework. However, there was probably further work on the superstructure of the north gate in 1511–12, once the adjacent hall had been completed, since the treasurer's accounts record payments to the mason John Lockhart for his work on what was described as the upper parts of the great tower in the northern corner of the castle. This is likely to have involved the construction of two great fireplaces on the first floor which, on account of the slope of the land, was at the level of the hall basement, while servery hatches were formed in the wall on the side towards the hall (**27**).

There must also have been a link building between the kitchen and the hall but, although there is still a connecting arch at the point

28 *The kitchen range, with its display showing the preparation of food in the sixteenth century.*

where the two buildings come closest to each other, it is no longer clear what form this link building took. It was perhaps as part of the same operation that a two-storeyed lean-to corridor range was constructed at the northern end of the hall, and it was presumably through these corridors that the food was brought from the kitchens into the hall. The vault over the transe along the west side of the hall may also have been a product of this campaign.

However, the kitchens above the north gate can never have been sufficient for the needs of the great hall on the most demanding occasions, and an extensive range of kitchens also had to be constructed to the north-east of the gate. These ran along the inside of the main curtain-wall on the side overlooking Gowan

Hill (**28**). The vaulting over these kitchens was removed, and the kitchens themselves infilled in 1689, when an artillery battery was constructed above them on this less naturally defended side of the castle. It was only as late as 1921 that the kitchens were partly reopened and the vaults reconstructed (**29**). So far as we can now understand them, there was a kitchen with a pair of fireplaces at the end of the range furthest away from the north gate. There was then a room which was presumably for the preparation of food, followed by a bakehouse which had two large ovens at the back of another double fireplace. Closest to the north gate was a room which may have been simply a storage cellar, though it now has a building above it that has served variously as the master gunner's house and as the quarters of the barrack warden, and the way this building was inserted within existing walls confuses the evidence.

29 *The kitchen range in the course of excavation in 1921*

All of these kitchens were interconnected by a spacious corridor on their western side, which may then have connected with the kitchens above the north gate. However, by the time it is depicted on the earliest surviving surveys of the castle, of the late seventeenth century, the area to the east of the hall was enclosed by walls and was referred to as the King's Office Houses. This suggests that, if necessary, food could be taken across the open area to the hall with little disturbance from other traffic, and that there was in fact little use of the road that crossed the area, leading through the north gate into the nether bailey.

The Chapel Royal

There is inevitably much that we still do not know about James IV's buildings in the castle, and this is particularly the case when we move on to consider the Chapel Royal. To add a further element of confusion, it becomes evident at this period that there must have been two church buildings within the castle, because both the treasurer's accounts and the Exchequer Rolls include references not only to the Chapel Royal but also to an old kirk. Double provision in this way would not have been unusual in a major royal castle, and we know that Edinburgh Castle also had two churches; however, while at Edinburgh we know exactly where they both were, this is not strictly true of either building at Stirling at this period.

Whatever the uncertainties, however, we can be in no doubt that James IV was determined that the services and religious rituals that took place within the chapel should be of a magnificence far outreaching that of any other royal chapel in the country. By no later than the 1490s he was at work assembling an appropriate body of clergy, and endowing them wherever possible by prudently diverting funds from other ecclesiastical establishments, including a number of religious houses and parish churches. On 2 May 1501 the pope, Alexander VI, gave his approval for the clergy to be formed into a collegiate body dedicated to St Mary and St Michael, which was to consist of a dean, a subdean, a sacrist, sixteen canons and six choristers.

Colleges of this type were incorporations of clergy attached to a particular church, and their main function was usually to pray for the welfare of their founders in life and for the salvation of their souls after death. Many great families founded such colleges near their principal residences, and several had already been set up by members of Scotland's royal family, though that at Stirling was to be the grandest of all. As first constituted, the dean was to have been the head of the earlier Chapel Royal of St Mary on the Rock in St Andrews, but it was later decided that the dean should be no less a person than the Bishop of Galloway, whose cathedral was at Whithorn. The college continued to grow over the years, and eventually the number of canons may have been increased to as many as twenty-eight, which made it by far the largest college ever set up in Scotland.

The vestments and furnishings that were provided to create an appropriate setting for the services within the chapel were evidently as impressive as they could be. We know from an inventory of 1505 that it was amply provided with vestments of all the colours appropriate for the liturgical seasons. There were also rich furnishings, including such items as a pewter gilt crucifix and brass candlesticks. The wooden choir-stalls must have attracted particular attention, because in 1506 they were specified as the model that was to be copied for new stalls being made for Glasgow Cathedral.

They presumably had elaborate canopies, and it is a possibility that a small fragment of elaborately carved cresting, now in the Smith Museum at Stirling, came from them or from some other part of the chapel furnishings.

The services could be accompanied by no less than three pairs of organs. These organs would have been similar to that shown on the altarpiece in the Scottish National Gallery which was painted around the late 1470s by Hugo van der Goes for Trinity College Chapel in Edinburgh, a college founded by James's grandmother, Queen Mary of Guelders. One of the greatest glories of the music must have been the settings for the services specially composed by Robert Carver, a canon of the Augustinian abbey of Scone. A number of pieces of his music have come down to us, and are increasingly often performed; they are among the finest works of their kind.

Since we know so much about the constitution of the college and about the worship that took place within it, it is rather galling that there are so many uncertainties about the structure itself, though we do have some clues to its position within the castle. A chapel certainly had to be orientated, so that its high altar was at the east end of the building. Bearing in mind the position of James's other buildings, his lodging and the hall, it also seems likely that he would have wished it to be on the north side of the main close of the castle, where the present chapel stands. But that building was only built to the form we now see in 1594.

As has already been said, however, there are the foundations of earlier buildings on a diagonal alignment below the present chapel, and the balance of possibilities suggests some of those represent the chapel in use in the time of James III (see **12, 13, 14**). It is most unlikely that James IV would have intended to have his own chapel in precisely the position indicated by those foundations. This is both because such a diagonally aligned building would be in conflict with the more regular planning for this part of the castle that he was evidently aiming for, and because it

30 *The head of a statue or effigy of a bishop, found in excavations at the east end of the Chapel Royal in 1986.*

probably postponed rebuilding the chapel because his father had already built or adapted one that was still of adequate scale to serve until something better could be built. The chapel which is perhaps represented by the later foundations below the north side of the courtyard, and which has already been discussed above, would certainly have been of ample scale; its main disadvantage was that it was in an awkward position. Unfortunately, however, as a result of James IV's premature death at the age of forty on the field of Flodden, his likely ambitions to build a more conveniently placed chapel in due course were never to be fulfilled.

Nevertheless, we learn from the surviving accounts that he certainly did something to make the existing chapel more suitable for its expanded functions. He spent money on the roof and what was probably an elaborate ceiling in 1494 and 1497, and paid £10 for work on the altar in 1497. A fine carved head of a bishop that was found during excavations at the east end of the chapel in 1986, and which seems likely to date from around the early sixteenth century, may also have been part of the works carried out for him at this time (**30**). The king's activities were apparently confirmed in a letter to the pope, of about 1501, in which he said he had renovated and adorned the chapel of the Blessed Mary and St Michael.

The forework

Because of the way the defensive perimeter walls of the castle had to follow the natural configuration of the top of the rock, its overall plan is rather complex. The main royal buildings we have considered in the earlier part of this chapter formed a roughly quadrangular grouping on a sloping platform at the highest level of the rock; but they were themselves within, and towards the west side of, a larger area forming the main enclosure of the castle. On a slightly lower platform to the north of this main enclave was a second elongated enclosure, the nether bailey, which communicated with the

must have obscured the main entrance to the hall which was under construction at this time. Yet, despite all of this, we do know from archaeological evidence that the building represented by those foundations continued to exist well into the sixteenth century, because a drain around its south-east corner was provided even after the vault had been built over the sunken corridor in front of the great hall.

Taking all of this into account, therefore, what seems likely is that, when James started work in earnest at Stirling Castle, he first concentrated on providing the buildings that were most urgently required: a lodging for himself and a more suitable hall than existed already. If this interpretation of the evidence is correct, he main area of the castle through the north gate. For much of the castle's history there was almost certainly an entrance into the nether bailey from the valley between the castle rock and Gowan Hill, and there may also have been a sally port on the west side of the nether bailey (see 57). But the main entrance to the castle must always have been from the south-east, where the sloping tail left by the action of the glacier on the volcanic rock not only made this side of the castle most vulnerable, but also provided the natural line of approach to it.

It was across this line that the strongest defences of the castle had to be ranged. By the same token, since this was the first part of the castle to be seen by those who approached it, this was also the side that set the architectural scene for the castle as a whole (31). To a king like James IV, who so obviously had a keen understanding of the messages that architecture

could be made to convey, it would be essential that the buildings on this side left those who came to the castle in no doubt about his own majesty. The forework built for him across this side, which partly occupies the line of earlier walls, was therefore a carefully articulated statement of both his power and his artistic tastes, as well as a defensive barrier. His new forework took the form of a high curtain-wall with a rectangular tower at each end and with the main gatehouse at its centre, the latter being flanked a short distance on each side by a half-round drum tower.

The curtain-wall itself was certainly thick enough to present a significant barrier to the artillery of the time, though we shall see that practical considerations were not the only ones in James's mind. This wall was capped by a crenellated (embattled) parapet carried on a decorative band of corbels (projecting stones). The rectangular towers at each end of the wall were of rather different sizes, that at the east end being significantly deeper towards the

31 *The forework, with the gatehouse to the right and the Prince's Tower to the left.*

32 *A conjectural reconstruction*
sketch of the forework (David Pollock).

north than its western counterpart, and a second length of curtain-wall stretched back from it to join up with the north gate. That east tower, which has come to be known as the Elphinstone Tower, may have housed the self-contained lodging of an important officer connected with the castle, and one of the rooms on the upper of the two surviving floors was apparently a kitchen. However, it was cut down in the later seventeenth century before any detailed views of it were drawn, and we do not know what was on the upper floors.

The western of the two rectangular towers, now usually known as the Prince's Tower, is set back slightly from the precipice on that side of the rock, and there was a short right-angled section of wall beyond it. That wall could have been part of either a pre-existing length of curtain-wall or of a building on that side, and it is tempting to suspect that it was the existence of a building there which resulted in this tower being less deep than its eastern counterpart. The Prince's Tower still stands almost to its original height,

apart from the tops of the crenellation around the wall-walk. It rises through three main storeys, with a garret within the roof that rises behind the parapet. It seems likely that the wall-head of the eastern tower would originally have terminated in a similar way.

The great focus of the forework was the lofty gatehouse near its central point which, like the Elphinstone Tower, has been greatly reduced over time (**colour plates 5, 6** and see **63**). Its main body was of rectangular plan with prominent three-quarter-round towers at the four angles, though the two inner ones have been demolished and the other two now only rise to less than half their original height. Of the semi-circular towers to each side of the gatehouse, no more than the base of one survives. But, despite these losses, from a combination of what remains of the flanking towers and Slezer's views of the later seventeenth century (see **22**), we can still appreciate that their contribution was important in the dramatic build-up of elements to the gatehouse itself (**32**).

The king and his masons were prepared to draw on a wide range of ideas for this frontispiece to his favourite castle, and while we cannot be certain what all of these were, we can at least speculate. The gatehouse itself was unusually wide for such a structure, and this allowed space for a symmetrical arrangement of entrances, with the centrally placed carriageway flanked by a pedestrian passage on each side. It would not have been unusual for a castle of this date to have a carriageway flanked by a single pedestrian passageway, but a symmetrical arrangement of this type was almost unheard of at the turn of the fifteenth and sixteenth centuries, though it was to be found some years later in the gateways of Henry VIII's Whitehall Palace. In some ways the effect may be compared to the triplet of portals common as the entrance to important medieval churches and found in some monastic gatehouses, and there may have been comparable processional requirements. It has also been suggested that there may have been some influence from the city gateways of Classical and Renaissance Italy. An intriguing feature is the way the designer of the arches framing these entrance ways has created a counterpoint between rounded and squared elements. The arches themselves are semicircular, but they are set back within square recessed heads which cut across the radiating stones of the arches, and a little above those frames are rectangular hood mouldings.

The design of the forework is strikingly medieval in vocabulary. Looking even at what remains, it is hard not to recall James's love of jousting and his evident fascination by the idealized cult of honour represented by the Arthurian legends. It is also significant that, although the main curtain-wall is relatively thick, and the gatehouse is provided with shot-holes for small hand-held guns, the forework as a whole by no means represents state-of-the-art fortification of the early sixteenth century. In particular, the walls of the gatehouse itself are thinner than might have been expected,

though this is a comforting demonstration of the fact that the king felt little pressing need for overwhelmingly strong defences here at the heart of his kingdom. Taking account of all of this, it seems possible that what was being built for him as the foretaste of his castle at Stirling was as much a statement of his own proud lineage and his wish to evoke the sense of a glorious chivalric past as it was a defensive barrier.

A similar self-consciously medieval vocabulary was probably also displayed in the towered outwork, known as the outer great bulwark, that James added in front of the east entrance to Linlithgow Palace. Little above the lower walls remains of that work, though it was evidently even less of a serious obstacle to would-be assailants than was Stirling's forework. But Stirling and Linlithgow were by no means alone in this creation of idealized castles. In his patronage of such buildings James was reflecting an awareness of an emerging taste for certain elements of historic architecture which was an important aspect of the intellectual framework of the northern Renaissance. Soaring towers with smaller turrets at their angles, like those of the gatehouse, were again becoming an increasingly prominent constituent of the architecture of major royal or noble residences in many parts of Europe, whether to contain their principal accommodation, or to give prestige to the main entrance. They were, incidentally, also to be a focus of some of the Tudor palaces of England. While defensibility was certainly a factor in their design, and the Stirling gate was itself equipped with portcullises and a retractable bridge of some form, there is much more to them than that.

In the case of the details of the Stirling gatehouse, it was perhaps France that was a leading source of inspiration. The basic form of the rectangular main mass with its circular angle towers may have been inspired by such examples as the late fourteenth-century donjon at Vincennes in the royal domain of France, though similar ideas were also to be taken up in England, as at Nunney in Somerset. Perhaps the most markedly French feature was the treatment of the wall-head. As with the stair cap-houses of the great hall, the walkway was carried around turreted cap-houses to create *chemins-de-ronde*, a feature which, although copied elsewhere in Europe, was particularly characteristic of French military architecture. It may be mentioned here that the Stirling gatehouse was later in its turn to be an influence on parts of the palaces at Falkland and Holyrood as rebuilt by James V in the late 1520s and 1530s.

The building accounts are not complete enough to allow us to date the forework as fully as might be wished, and it would be particularly useful to know when work had started. Nevertheless, there are a number of pointers to the progress of the work in its later stages. References to operations on the foretower in 1501 by the mason John Yorkston, and to the kitchen tower in 1503, probably by the same mason, are likely to refer to parts of the forework. The mason John Lockhart, whom we have already seen at work on the north gate, was probably the person in charge of the gatehouse itself, and enough was complete on that by 1504 for the portcullis to be installed. The final payments for the gate of the 'forewerk' would seem to have been in 1506. Both of those masons were then involved in completing the curtain-wall between the towers.

James IV's other building works at the castle

It is important to remember that, while all this building activity was under way, life in the castle was continuing at its normal pace. The accounts are full of references to the activities that made royal life bearable. Plants, seeds and trees were being bought for the gardens; grapes were being transported from Ayr for the royal table; in the chapel the organs were being repaired and there was work on the Easter sepulchre and paschal candlestick; morris dancers were being paid; tapestries and feather beds were being carried to and from the castle, together with a tub for the king's closet on one occasion; fish were being provided for the ponds. Major reconstruction was such a fact of life at the royal residences of this period that one is left with the impression that it was simply disregarded by the principal occupants.

James IV also ordered improvements to the parkland associated with the castle. He apparently revived the Old Park, immediately below and to the south of the castle walls, in preference to the New Park some distance to its south where Robert I's army had sheltered before Bannockburn in 1314. Sir Harry Wood was evidently much involved in this re-creation, presumably reconstructing the ditches and palisaded banks which prevented the escape of game. We also have fascinating insights into the transportation to the park of deer from as far away as Falkland, while we know that by 1509 white cattle were roaming within it, perhaps like those still in the High Park at Hamilton. James's love of horsemanship was demonstrated not only by the hunting that took place within the park, but equally by a display of the prowess of a troop of Spanish horsemen in 1509.

The accounts suggest that James IV's architectural activities can have left few parts of the castle entirely untouched, though we now know very little about a number of his building projects. As already hinted, a particular mystery is the whereabouts of the accommodation provided for his queen, Margaret Tudor, after their marriage in 1503. A queen expected to be housed with due state, in deference to her own high standing as a representative of a foreign nation, and would thus be provided with a distinct lodging of her own. At Holyrood, for example, James and Margaret each had a lodging consisting of a sequence of hall, a great chamber and an inner chamber, and there would probably also have been smaller closets beyond.

33 *The Ladies' Hole, overlooking the gardens and park.*

At Stirling, while there are enigmatic references to her chamber in the accounts for 1504, there are no indications of where this was. However, bearing in mind that the king's own lodging was almost certainly on the west side of the inner close, in the King's Old Building, it is probable that the queen's lodging would have been nearby, though it may have been no more than a refurbishment of an existing range of lodgings. Perhaps the most likely situation for it is somewhere in the area now occupied by the palace built for James V, and the architectural evidence of the palace clearly demonstrates that some earlier buildings on the site were retained and incorporated into its lowest storey when it was built. It has already been mentioned that the Prince's Tower, at the west end of the forework, is set back from the cliff edge, leaving space for a length of wall beyond it, which turns to run towards the King's Old Building (see **37**). Though it can be

no more than speculation, it is one possibility that this was part of the queen's lodging, particularly since its west wall is on a roughly parallel alignment with the back wall of the King's Old Building itself. An alternative situation for the queen's lodging might be below the north range of the later palace, in which situation it would have the advantage for James IV's replanning of the castle's main enclosure that it defined the side of the close across from the chapel.

It is worth mentioning that to the west of the palace is an irregular walled area which was known by 1584 as the Ladies' Hole, and from where it is said that the ladies of the court looked down on to the park, gardens and tilting yards in the valley below (**33**). Could it be that the area acquired this use when the ladies of the queen's household were attending Queen Margaret in an adjacent lodging either on the west or the north side of where the palace now stands? It would be attractive to think of the display of the Spanish riders being watched by the ladies from there in 1509.

CHAPTER THREE

The royal residence completed

James V and Stirling

After the disaster of the battle of Flodden in 1513, the newly widowed Queen Margaret Tudor took her seventeen-month-old son to her castle of Stirling. It was in the Chapel Royal that he was crowned as James V on 21 September (34). While she was resident at Stirling she also gave birth to James IV's posthumous son, Alexander Duke of Ross, who was to die before he reached the age of two. Under the terms of her husband's will, Margaret had become guardian of the young king and was thus well placed to be effective head of state; though, as the sister of Henry VIII of England, whose forces had killed James IV and so many of his nobility at Flodden, she was never likely to have been popular. She sealed her own political fate when, less than a year after her husband's death, she married Archibald Earl of Angus, head of the Douglas family, and in so doing lost the right to be guardian of her sons.

The council urged John Duke of Albany (next in line to the throne after the children of the marriage of James IV and Margaret Tudor) to hasten to Scotland to take up the regency. He was a grandson of James II, and had been brought up in France following an abortive rebellion by his father, Duke Alexander, against James III. Albany eventually reached Scotland in 1515, despite the efforts of the English to prevent him, and dramatic stories are told of how the queen mother refused to give up her children when the duke's messengers arrived for them at Stirling. In this she was supported by Lord Drummond, the keeper of the castle, who was her new husband's grandfather. But she was forced to hand them over when the duke himself came at the head of a besieging army of over 7000 men and a train of guns which included the famous bombard

34 *James V (by permission, Scottish National Portrait Gallery).*

Mons Meg. Margaret and her husband found it convenient to take refuge in England for a while as a consequence.

The following years cannot have been a happy time for the young king as various factions struggled for control of him. It is hardly surprising that he was later described by George Buchanan, the tutor of James VI, as being of a 'naturally suspicious disposition'. Nevertheless, he probably received a better education than is often suggested. For some time he was taught by Gavin Dunbar, who was referred to as preceptor of the king in 1518, at a time when he was dean of the diocese of Moray; Dunbar was eventually rewarded by being made Archbishop of Glasgow in 1523. James was also educated within Stirling by John Lord Erskine, father of the first Earl of Mar, who was by then the keeper of the castle. But in 1524, following the final departure for France of the Duke of Albany, his mother regained control of both the royal person and the kingdom for a short period, and it seems that less attention may then have been given to his education.

The king's situation worsened from 1525. In that year it was decided that each of the leading nobles should take a turn in looking after him; but Angus, who was by then estranged from the queen mother, refused to hand over the king at the end of his term of custody and kept him a virtual prisoner. According to Buchanan, Angus and his family encouraged the young king's taste for women, in the hope of strengthening their hold over him. Eventually, in 1528, when he was sixteen, he escaped to Stirling Castle where he showed considerable astuteness in establishing his own authority, and also began to demonstrate his implacable loathing of the family that had held him against his will. In the following year the queen mother agreed to hand over possession of Stirling Castle to her son, in exchange for lands elsewhere.

As the king's authority grew over the following years, it became apparent that two of his greatest concerns were to circumscribe the power of his nobles and to build up a secure financial base for the crown. Both of these aims are eminently understandable in view of his own early experiences. He had personally suffered badly from the ambitions of one noble family, the Douglases, and history showed all too clearly how the minorities of several of his predecessors had been similarly clouded by attempts to gain control of the kingdom through possession of an infant king. On the second score, by the time he assumed authority the crown was desperately short of funds as a result of the profligacy of his mother and step-father, while the periods of Scottish residence of Regent Albany had also been extremely expensive. As an inevitable result of the policies James consequently pursued, he came to be regarded extremely warily by many of the nobility, who could find themselves targets of both his suspicion and his acquisitiveness.

Despite his seemingly arbitrary behaviour towards many of the nobility, however, it seems he was rather better liked by many of the ordinary people of his kingdom, and one illustration of this is particularly associated with Stirling. It is said that he used to pass among his subjects so that he could hear of their needs at first hand, and so that he would not be recognized he dressed as one of them, eventually coming to be known as the 'gudeman of Ballengeich' (Ballengeich is the valley between the castle and Gowan Hill). This delightfully improbable story is no more than a legend, though there is evidence that James did have an interest in organizing the judicial system more effectively. In 1532 he set up a college of justice, with Abbot Alexander Myln of Cambuskenneth as its first president, though this was only the first and rather ineffective stage in a long process. The chief funding for this college was found by an unprecedented level of taxation of the Church's assets, in which he was able to count on the support of a pope who was deeply worried that Scotland would follow England along the path to Reformation.

James reacted against the strongly English orientation of his mother and stepfather by looking even more towards Europe than had many of his predecessors, and the natural friend in any alliance against England was still France. The way for a closer relationship had already been paved by Regent Albany, whose Treaty of Rouen of 1517 sought to cement the alliance by marrying James to a daughter of the French king, François I. François himself showed some reluctance to put this into effect, but the fear of James allying himself instead with either the emperor, Charles V, or even with England, eventually produced the desired result. James went to France in July 1536, and was rewarded with the hand of the Princess Madeleine, whom he married in Paris on 1 January 1537. While in France he evidently paid some attention to the architecture of the country, taking advantage of the presence in his train of his French master mason Mogin Martin, who had accompanied him from Scotland. He may also have been accompanied by Sir James Hamilton of Finnart, on whom he was soon to rely in several of his building operations.

James's sixteen-year-old wife was to die within six months of their marriage, but less than a year after that he remarried, and again reinforced the French alliance in doing so. This second time he married Mary of Guise-Lorraine, the highly capable eldest daughter of Claude Duke of Guise, and widow of the Duke of Longueville. Such high-born French ladies had to be accommodated in the manner to which they were accustomed if the prestige of the Scottish crown were to be maintained, though it might have been thought that the major building operations carried out for James IV would have made this easily possible.

However, it has been suggested in the previous chapter that, despite all the building work he instigated, it is unlikely that James IV had been able to carry through to completion all of his plans for Stirling Castle before his premature death on the field of Flodden in 1513. James V was to die yet more prematurely in 1542, when he was only thirty, and thus had even less time to devote to building operations than his father. Nevertheless, despite his short lifespan, he carried out a prodigious amount of palace building, and at Holyrood and Falkland his work was even more prominent than that of his father, while he also spent a great deal of money at Linlithgow. But it is at Stirling that we see his single most impressive building, the great quadrangular palace that rises behind his father's forework.

The palace

After James V assumed personal control of his kingdom there was a further change in the royal accounting processes. From 1529 onwards the fullest references to the king's building operations began to be recorded in the accounts of the Masters of Works rather than in the accounts of the Lord High Treasurer. Even so, there are still many gaps in the records and, regrettably for our purposes, the greatest of these lacunae is the accounts for the building operations on the palace (**colour plate 7**).

Among the earliest expenditure on building that we hear of at the castle in the time of James V was a considerable amount on a stable below the castle in 1531–2. At the same time there was also work on a number of presumably more prestigious buildings, including the king's 'great chamber where he eats', his outer chamber, his chamber, his wardrobe, his kitchen and his kitchen 'dressory', the last of these being presumably for the preparation of food. All of these could refer to rooms in the King's Old Building. There are also references to works on the queen's outer chamber, the great hall, a room referred to as the 'dusty hall', the chapel, and to accommodation for various office holders. The master of works for most of these operations was Sir James Nicholson, a chaplain, who was at first answerable to John Scrymgeour. It is interesting to note at this time that there begin to be references to a palace, though this probably should not be taken to mean that work on the new palace itself had been started.

As we shall see, a number of the details of the palace suggest it was designed by one of the king's foreign masons, and more probably by one of French origin (see 38). There were certainly several foreign craftsmen in the king's service around the time the palace must have been under construction. Among those of French origin were the masons Nicholas Roy, John Roytell, Moses (or Mogin) Martin, the carver Andrew Mansioun, the painter Piers and the organ builder Gillean. Individuals who could have been of Netherlandish origin included Patrick Fleming and Peter Flemishman. However, there was also one very important person of Scottish origin who played a major if now undefinable part in the construction of the palace, and that was Sir James Hamilton of Finnart.

Hamilton of Finnart was a bastard son of the first Earl of Arran of the Hamilton family, who was born some time around 1500, and who was executed for reasons which still remain uncertain in 1540. Until immediately before his death he enjoyed great royal favour. We know that the king particularly relied on him in his architectural operations and, as has already been said, he may have accompanied James on his marriage trip to France in 1536–7. He had been very closely involved in the royal building works at Linlithgow Palace and Blackness Castle from 1534, for example, though his interest in building had been evident even earlier than that at his own castle of Craignethan in Lanarkshire and at his family's castle of Cadzow, near Hamilton.

It is unclear when Hamilton first became involved at Stirling, but it is likely to have been around the time that James's French marriages in 1537 and 1538 gave the construction of a suitable palace particular urgency. In support of this, the accounts of the masters of works for 1537–8 refer slightly portentously to payments for work that had been carried out at

the castle 'before Sir James Hamilton's entry thereto', suggesting that his appearance on the scene was a major watershed in the operations. His important role in the work is also suggested by two other documents. On 22 September 1539 the register of the great seal includes a charter by which Hamilton received grants or confirmation of property in part recompense for the completion of works on the palaces of Linlithgow and Stirling. In the same year the register of the privy seal records his appointment as principal master of works throughout the realm, and from the extent of his involvement in the royal works it is clear that this was no honorary post.

We cannot be certain how far he was involved in the design process at the Stirling palace, and opinions vary widely. I believe that his role was probably essentially that of an agent who had a particularly clear idea of what he wanted on his royal master's behalf, together with a strong presumption that his wishes would be respected. The strikingly wide range of architectural solutions adopted in the buildings with which he was involved, together with the great variety in the planning, do not seem to be consistent with the idea that his could have been the creative mind behind them all.

The designer of the Stirling palace faced some daunting difficulties, to which he responded magnificently. The land on which it was to be set sloped quite steeply down from west to east; there were already buildings on the site which were to be at least partly absorbed into the new work; it was also necessary to fit the building in so that it abutted James IV's forework on one side, and presented impressive faces both to the lower close immediately within the forework and to the inner close on the rock summit (35). In his favour, however, the designer had the advantage that the type of accommodation required was relatively limited. Whereas at Linlithgow, Holyrood and Falkland the design of the palaces had to embrace the major spaces of great hall and chapel within the overall scheme, at Stirling both of these already existed

35 *The palace and forework.*

as free-standing buildings elsewhere in the castle. The main requirement for the new palace was essentially a pair of conjoined lodgings for the king and his queen, though there were also some basement rooms below, as well as lodgings in an attic storey that were probably for officers of state.

The royal lodgings were set out so that they spread around three sides of a rectangular open courtyard, which was sometimes referred to as the Lion's Den. (This name could refer to the chief element in the Scottish royal heraldry, and heraldic beasts were certainly placed along the skyline of the palace roofs (36); however, a lion is known to have been bought for the king in Flanders in 1537, and it is a possibility it may sometimes have been housed here.) The

lodgings were entered at the western end of the façade towards the inner close, where there may have been a porch that has since been replaced by a rather smaller structure (see 58). On account of the higher ground levels at the top end of the upper square there was no basement below the palace at this point, so that, rather unusually, the main floor of the building was entered directly at the level of the royal lodgings, with no need of a stair.

There were three main rooms in each lodging, which decreased in size as they became progressively more private and generally less accessible. The names of the rooms were to vary through time, but it is likely the sequence was an outer hall, followed by a great or outer chamber (which might also be known as an inner hall) and then an inner chamber. The inner chambers intercommunicated with each

36 *A lion finial from one of the gables of the palace.*

was a gallery in the west range; it had a doorway flanked by pairs of windows looking down into the Lion's Den. This gallery was originally higher than we now see, and when the lower ceiling was inserted the windows and doorway towards the Lion's Den were reduced in size. The range as a whole may also have been reduced in width, possibly after one survey of 1583 revealed that the roof of this side of the palace was collapsing, while another of 1625 reported that part of its foundations had fallen over the cliff. However, on the evidence of the way that a stump of earlier work seems to have been retained in modified form at the southern end of the range, it is also possible that this side of the palace was never finished as originally planned (**37**). On the opposite side of the palace from the west gallery, and leading off the king's outer chamber, a bridge over the road between the lower and inner

other. There were also small closets to each lodging, where the royal couple could enjoy the greatest seclusion from the pressures of the court. One of these in each case was perhaps a small study or cabinet, while another may possibly have contained a more comfortable bed than the great bed in the inner chamber. One would also have contained the royal close-stool and bathtub. The king's closets were in a small lean-to range along the east side of the Lion's Den, and were reached from his inner chamber; they also contained a small stair leading to the attic floor. From the evidence of eighteenth-century plans it seems the queen's closets were in a narrow range behind the fore-work wall, running from the south-east corner of the palace towards the gatehouse, though they no longer survive. From the southern end of the queen's closets there was also access to an elevated terrace behind the parapet of the wall-walk, running back to the Prince's Tower.

Connecting the halls of the two lodgings, and reached directly from the main entrance,

37 *The south-west corner of the palace, showing the retained stretch of earlier work.*

38 *The palace towards the lower close.*

closes was constructed to give direct access to the dais of the great hall. The present bridge is a charming neo-Gothic structure, probably of later eighteenth-century date, but traces of the earlier bridge can still be seen on both the palace and the hall.

The rooms in the attic storey of the palace were probably initially destined for use as additional accommodation by officers of state. They were not intended to be visible from the outside of the palace block, and were lit by dormer windows behind the parapet on at least some of the outer faces of the palace, as well as by windows looking down into the Lion's Den. One of the greatest physical changes to the palace took place when an apartment was formed in the attic storey for the governor of the castle in the years around 1700. A series of highly disruptive large windows was cut through the outer walls of the

palace to light it (38), while the wall-head towards the Lion's Den was heightened and the windows were increased in number and enlarged. A little later, in the earlier decades of the eighteenth century, the original porch was replaced by a smaller structure, which was combined with a stair that afforded more imposing access to the governor's apartment than had at first been provided (see 58).

The most memorable feature of the palace is its series of external façades. These display a fascinating blend of ideas, in which are to be seen some of the earliest examples of the impact of Renaissance architecture anywhere in Britain. Towards the inner close and behind the forework only the principal storey is given architectural expression, but towards the lower close the basement is allowed to be seen as a itself is crenellated (embattled), a type of wall-head treatment that still tended to be regarded as *de rigueur* on many high-status buildings, and which probably also echoed the wall-head treatment of the other buildings around the inner close, helping to give that area a degree of homogeneity.

There is nothing quite like the Stirling palace façades elsewhere, and it is difficult to know from where the inspiration for the complex intermixture of medieval and Classical ideas could have come. Indeed, it is possible the designing masons were themselves only partly conscious of the sources of their ideas though, as with the design of James IV's forework, it is worth considering some of the possibilities. The idea for the cusped arches and the baluster shafts could have come from France, where they are seen in different contexts in buildings of comparable grandeur such as those parts of the royal palace of Blois built by Louis XII; as already said, we do know that several French masons were working in Scotland, so this is certainly possible. The alternation of windows and statuary, and the complex upward and outward stepping of the façade may show a more distant awareness of what was happening in parts of Italy. There a number of architects were trying to break free of what they increasingly saw as the strait-jacket of the

39 *A representation of a soldier with a crossbow from the south parapet of the palace.*

full storey (**38**). The rich surface modelling of the palace façades is remarkable for the way that they step backwards and forwards in a series of raised and recessed sections. Slightly unexpectedly, the rectangular windows are in the raised rather than the recessed sections, where they are capped by segmental tympana within relieving arches, in which I5 is carved, in reference to the king ('Iacobus 5'). The recessed sections are bridged at a higher level than the window-heads by segmental arches decorated with dropped cusping, and within each of the arches is a statue on a richly carved two-stage baluster shaft. Above these arches, in front of the parapet, are smaller statues on shafts (**39**). The two main storeys are demarcated by a horizontal string course, with winged angel heads carved in its lower hollow. This horizontal line is echoed in an even heavier string course below the wall-head parapet, which also has winged angels. The parapet

40 *One of the figurative corbels of the palace.*

strict Classical rules of architecture, by placing the standard elements in new relationships with each other. This led to the development of the type of self-consciously wilful designs that are now generally described as 'Mannerist', and there could be something of this in the Stirling palace. The rather busy alternation of windows and statuary recesses, for example, was to have counterparts across Europe from Rome to Heidelberg, albeit always retranslated into the local architectural dialect.

Alongside such modern ideas, it is also just conceivable that in the basic form of the palace, with its massive rectangular shape, its strong pilaster-like projections at regular intervals and its crenellated parapet, its designer was casting a backward glance at the keeps or donjons of earlier royal castles in England and on the Continent. Such buildings often still carried great prestige, being carefully maintained as symbols of royal authority within many castles, and it is therefore not impossible that, among his other aims, James wished to present something of this same impression. Perhaps to an even greater extent than in our own age, the presentation of a correct image was highly important in the sixteenth century.

Much of the impression of architectural richness which strikes anyone who looks at the palace comes from the sculpture, which must have been the work of several craftsmen. Apart from the elaborate string courses already referred to, horizontally projecting figures, some of which are portrayed with such realism that they could be representations of members of the court, support the main balusters (**40**). They are reflected in more grotesque images acting as corbels at the springings of the arches along the façades and below the upper statuary, the latter also serving as waterspouts. But the greatest efforts were concentrated on the two tiers of statues. The statue at the north-east corner was clearly intended to be a portrait of the king himself (**41**). Many of the others are unidentifiable, though they include a splendidly hermaphroditic devil (**42**) and some robustly

41 *The statue of James V at the north-east corner of the palace.*

buxom beauties who are evidently Classical goddesses. The interest in scholarship that was expected at the court of a Renaissance king is also displayed in the inclusion of some of the planetary deities, which were copied from engravings by Hans Burgkmair.

It may be assumed that the interiors of the royal lodgings would have depended largely on costly hangings and furnishings for their effect. The main focus of each is now a fireplace, with lintels carried on massive rounded or square shafts, and with delightful capitals in which animals, birds and cherubs are grouped so as to reflect the basic form of Corinthian capitals (**43**). In the inner chambers the smaller-scale fireplaces were additionally enriched by panels of recessed carving on the shafts. An even greater contribution to the appearance of the rooms was originally made by the ceilings of at least some of them. They were decorated by

42 *A representation of the devil from the south face of the palace.*

44 *One of the oak roundels from the ceiling of the royal apartments in the palace.*

43 *The fireplace in the Queen's Outer Hall of the palace.*

carved-oak roundels containing heads or figures, which were taken down in 1777 because they were no longer safe (44). Thirty-eight of these survive in whole or in part, but there were originally more and they evidently formed part of a complex decorative scheme. An engraving of 1817 published in a book about them called *Lacunar Strevelinense* shows them as set within a rectilinear grid of mouldings (45). We do not know if this engraving is based on evidence or if it was merely guesswork on the part of its author, though it has been pointed out that such an arrangement would have similarities with the decoration of the stone ceiling above the stair in the French château of Azay-le-Rideau (near Tours). It is possible that some of the ceilings would have been of different designs, and surviving ceilings of the period at both the palaces of Falkland and Holyrood have mouldings set out to a variety of more elaborate geometrical patterns.

Such roundels are an essentially Classical motif, and are to be seen in several French buildings of the Renaissance, and also at Hampton Court in England. Similar roundels (although in stone rather than timber) were also being applied to the façades of the palace that was remodelled and enlarged for James at Falkland from 1537. It could thus be significant that the wright (carpenter) Robert Robertson, who came to work at Stirling in 1541, had earlier worked at Falkland. As with the statuary on the outside of the Stirling palace, however, there is no doubt that several carvers were at work on carving the roundels. Among other craftsmen who could have been involved are the king's master wright John Drummond, who is specifically linked with the palace ceilings in a history of the Drummond family written in 1681. The king's French carver Andrew Mansioun has also been suggested as someone who worked on the ceilings, and this could explain the similarities with French examples of such roundels. Some of the roundels show the same skill in portraying character that is to be seen in the stone corbels along the outside of the palace, and there is again a feeling that members of the court are being brought to life in them.

The appointment of Robert Robertson in 1541 to oversee the carpentry work in the castle may suggest that construction of the masonry shell of the palace had reached a stage when the emphasis could shift to the timberwork. By then Sir James Hamilton of Finnart had been executed and the master of works was once again Sir James Nicholson, who had held that post before Hamilton of Finnart swaggered on to the scene. Yet it is by no means certain that the shell of the palace was completed even by the death of James V in 1542, since it would have been an astonishingly speedy piece of construction to build such a large structure between Hamilton of Finnart's arrival at Stirling in 1538 and the king's death four years

45 *An engraving of 1817 showing one of the rooms in the palace with the ceiling roundels as they were thought to have been fitted (from* Lacunar Strevelinense).

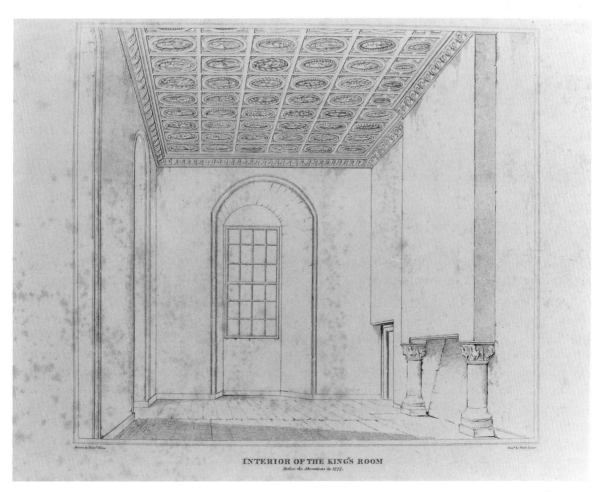

INTERIOR OF THE KING'S ROOM
Before the Alterations in 1777.

later. One tantalizing pointer to the possibility that the work continued after his death is a small gablet built into a terrace wall to the south of the Prince's Tower. It has the crowned initials M. R, in reference either to James V's widow, Queen Mary of Guise, or to their daughter, Mary Queen of Scots. This gablet clearly came from a dormer window, and traditionally it is said to have come from one of those on the palace. A similar gablet, of which all trace has now been lost, is said to have had the date 1557. If tradition is correct in associating these gablets with the palace, this suggests a rather less hurried campaign than is often assumed. Beyond this, as has already been said, the remains of earlier work at the south-west corner could suggest it never was completely finished (see 37).

Mary of Guise and Mary Queen of Scots

James V died at Falkland Palace on 14 December 1542. It is said that he died broken in spirit because of the total rout of his forces by the English at the battle of Solway Moss, and that he simply lay with his face to the wall until his end came. His daughter, Mary, had been born at Linlithgow six days previously, but that was of little comfort to him. He had already lost two baby sons, James and Arthur, in the previous year, and he is said to have entertained little hope for the continuity of his dynasty, which hung on the thread of the life of a baby girl less than one week old.

Soon after his death, relations between two of those who were governing the kingdom on her behalf, the Earl of Arran and Cardinal David Beaton, were already deteriorating, foreshadowing the years of conflict that were to follow through her minority. In all of this Henry VIII of England, who viewed Mary's minority as the best chance since the death of the Maid of Norway for England to establish authority over Scotland, was eagerly watching his opportunities. On 1 July 1543, after much

diplomacy, it was agreed by the Treaty of Greenwich that Mary should be betrothed to Henry's son, the five-year-old Prince Edward. But despite assurances that Scottish independence would be guaranteed, many Scots, and particularly those who feared that Scotland would be forced to follow England in breaking with the Catholic Church, were not happy about this. These fears were not diminished by Henry's less than tactful demands that the baby princess should be sent almost immediately to England. Cardinal Beaton, the senior prelate of the Scottish Church, and one of the most vehement of the anti-English party, instead decided that she should be taken to Stirling Castle for her own safety. This he put into effect himself, at the head of a considerable force, and once at Stirling Mary was placed under the care of Lord Erskine, who had earlier had responsibility for her father in his minority.

On 9 September 1543 the infant Mary was crowned within the Chapel Royal at Stirling. Henry VIII's representative, Sir Ralph Sadler, remarked dismissively that it was carried out 'with such solemnitie as they do use in this country, which is not very costlie'. (As a stroke of cruel irony, Sadler was later one of the commission which condemned Mary to death.) At the coronation the crown was carried by the Earl of Arran, the sceptre by the Earl of Lennox and the sword by the Earl of Argyll. However, the Earl of Lennox, who had claims to be the second most important person in the kingdom by virtue of his descent from James II, and who had plans to bolster his claims by marrying the daughter of Queen Margaret Tudor and the Earl of Angus, joined the pro-English party immediately after attending the coronation. Lennox was soon in open rebellion, the chief result of which was to be his own exile in England. By April 1544 Henry VIII realized that the prospect of the marriage of Mary and Edward was receding in the face of fears of English motives by the majority of Scots. He determined to force the issue, and in May an

1 *Stirling Castle, a distant view from the west.*   2 *Stirling Castle from the south-west.*

3 *Stirling Castle, an aerial view.*

4 *The battle of Bannockburn, as painted by Sir William Allen.*

5 *The forework gateway in 1800, by Walmsley and Cartwright.*   6 *The forework and palace.*

7 *The façade of the palace towards the inner close.*

8 *Stirling Castle in 1789, by A. Grant and J. Wells.*

9 *A temporary display showing medieval masons at work in the great hall.*

10 *Abbey Craig and the Wallace Monument.*

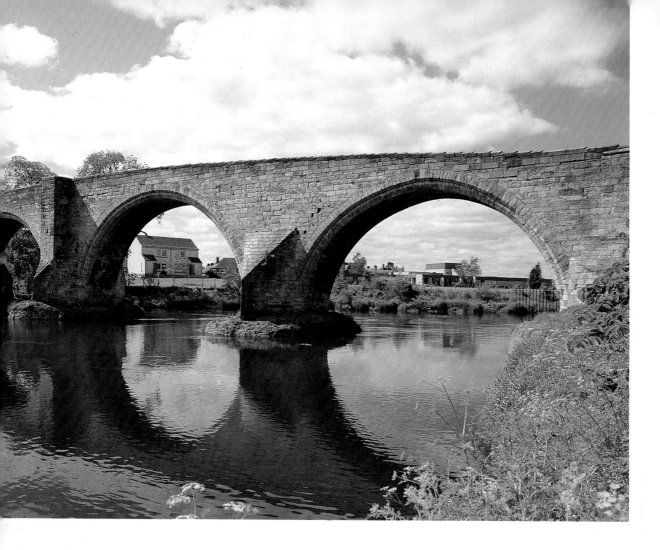

11 *Stirling bridge.*

12 *The parish church of the Holy Rude.*

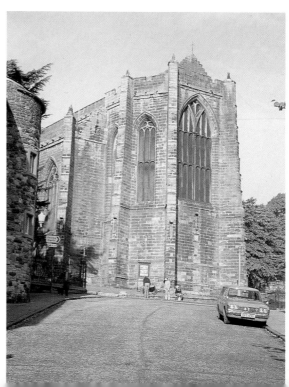

13 *The tower of Cambuskenneth Abbey, with Stirling Castle in the background.*

14 *Mar's Work.*

15 *Argyll's Lodging.*

invasion under the leadership of the Earl of Hertford came ashore near Edinburgh. This was the beginning of what has come to be known as the 'rough wooing' of Scotland. In an attempt to establish stronger rule over Scotland, in June 1544 the queen mother, Mary of Guise, was briefly declared governor of the kingdom in the place of the Earl of Arran, who was felt to be too weak, though Arran had again re-established his position by November.

By the death of Henry VIII in January 1547 the matter was no nearer a resolution that was satisfactory to the English. England was now ruled on behalf of the young Edward VI by the Duke of Somerset, who had been responsible for the earlier invasion of Scotland when Earl of Hertford. He launched a further onslaught in 1547, and about one week after crossing the border, a numerically weaker English force trounced a poorly equipped Scottish army at Pinkie on 10 September. The young queen was moved further beyond the reach of the English, from Stirling to the island priory of Inchmahome, where a son of Lord Erskine was commendator. Discussions soon opened on obtaining French help against the English. The price of French help was the betrothal of Mary to the dauphin François, the son of King Henri II and heir to the French throne, together with the immediate delivery of the young queen to the French. On balance this was regarded as a price worth paying, and she set sail for France from Dumbarton on 29 July 1548. She was to be absent from her kingdom for the next thirteen years, during which time she became Queen of France in 1559.

For much of the period of her absence southern Scotland was a battleground between the English and French, one incidental consequence of which was that a number of sophisticated artillery fortifications were built by the two opposing sides. The major castles of Edinburgh and Stirling were also eventually provided with new outworks which would allow the approaches to those castles to be defended by and from artillery, and it is now realized that

46 *The French Spur.*

substantial parts of what was built at Stirling still survive in modified form. There is a tradition that the outer defences pre-dating those now seen were built by the French troops of Mary of Guise, who had become regent of the kingdom on behalf of her absent daughter in April 1554. The date sometimes given is 1559, though work could have started some years before. The tradition of the French connection with this part of the castle was still sufficiently strong in about 1680 for Captain John Slezer to refer to one part of these defences as 'The French Spurre' on a plan he then drew. Corroboration of a French connection is to be seen in the tablet carved with a fleur-de-lis that is still prominently visible on its prow, though this could equally refer to Mary Queen of Scots, who was also Queen of France (**46**).

From plans, drawings and views made before major alterations of 1708–14 we know the main element of the defences was in the form of a large angled spur with a wide wall-walk behind (see **22** and **59**). At the prow of the spur the walls sloped inwards to form a pyramidal shape known as a talus, behind which the upper walls followed a curved line; at the centre of the curve was a sentry box, though this was probably a later addition. A ditch ran in front of the spur, except at its west end, where there was the ramped approach to the entrance gate of the castle, and that entrance was protected by a second and smaller spur to its west.

47 The remains of the prow of the artillery spur embodied in the wall to the right of the outer defences gateway.

But perhaps the most sophisticated feature of the whole design was another spur at the north-eastern end of the main spur, the part referred to by Slezer as the French spur. This was designed as a demi-bastion, which projected a short way in front of the end of the main spur as an ear-like shape known as an orillon, in the recess behind which were gun emplacements which could fire along the ditch and the east face of the spur. The north face of this demi-bastion may also have been intended to command the approaches to Stirling bridge, in the valley below the walls of the castle. In the design of this feature we come quite close to the spirit of the great bastioned fortifications that had been brought to perfection by the Italians, and that were now being widely used elsewhere (see **46**).

Suspicions that much of this work might survive have been confirmed by excavations carried out in 1977–8. These showed that the French Spur is largely intact, except that a wall has been built across the mouth of its inset flank (see **65**). It is also now clear that the east wall of the main spur still stands in modified form, and that a curved section of masonry to the north of the main gate was part of its prow (**47**). A fragment of the wall of the ramped approach road has also been found in the guardroom square, part of the inner wall of

the west spur has been tentatively identified within a later wall, and a wall which projects out from the Prince's Tower is probably the stump of the wall of the western spur where it abutted that tower (see **31**). We therefore now know that what first confronts modern visitors on their approach to Stirling Castle includes the substantial remains of an important early artillery work (**48**).

By the middle years of the sixteenth century, the Anglo-French hostilities that were being fought out over Scotland, and that resulted in the construction of such impressive artillery fortifications, took on a heightened religious dimension. Queen Mary of England, who had attempted to reintroduce Catholicism south of the border, had died in November 1558, and the Protestant party was again in the ascendant. By contrast, within Scotland, from March 1559 Mary of Guise was showing strengthened determination to suppress those who wished to overthrow the old Church. Her efforts took on greater urgency after the reformer John Knox returned to Scotland on 2 May, and began to preach a series of inflammatory sermons which gave the movement for reform a greater focus. In response to the growing threat, the government ordered that there should be a muster of troops at Stirling on 24 May. But the reforming party was gathering in strength, and in June marched from Perth to Edinburgh by way of Stirling, incidentally 'cleansing' the burgh's friaries *en route*.

Stirling continued to be an important centre of activity, and a convention meeting there on 10 September was joined six days later by the Earl of Arran (son of the previous Earl of Arran, who by then enjoyed the title of Duke of Chatelherault). From Stirling they marched on Edinburgh, but were forced to retreat when faced with Mary of Guise's superior forces, and it was at Stirling that Knox attempted to put spirit back into them. Despite this set-back, the future was to be with the reforming party. English troops had already entered Scotland in their support in March 1560, and the death of the queen mother on 11 June left the Catholic and pro-French party without a figurehead. Scotland became a 'reformed' nation when the parliament of August repudiated the authority of the pope and abolished the mass as the principal form of worship.

Mary Queen of Scots

François II of France died on 5 December 1560, leaving Mary a widow a few days before her eighteenth birthday. She quickly realized that her best prospects lay in returning to her Scottish kingdom, where she would be the reigning monarch, rather than in staying in France where she was now only queen dowager. After a suitable period of mourning and a somewhat troubled voyage, on 19 August 1561 she reached Scotland. Though she herself was to remain firmly Catholic, her kingdom was now Protestant, and she was to find herself being frequently reminded of this. A few weeks after her return she moved on from Holyrood to Stirling, where the Chapel Royal was by then the only one of the places of worship in the palaces that was still furnished for Catholic observances; indeed, an inventory of 1562 suggests that the impression given by the vestments and altar-hangings must still have been very rich, with sets in all the liturgical colours. But even in her chapel she was not to be allowed to worship in peace, and at high mass on the first Sunday of her stay at Stirling the Earl of Argyll and her half-brother Lord

48 *A drawing showing the existing outer defences (in heavy black line) with the mid-sixteenth-century artillery defences superimposed (in broken or thinner line) (Sylvia Stevenson).*

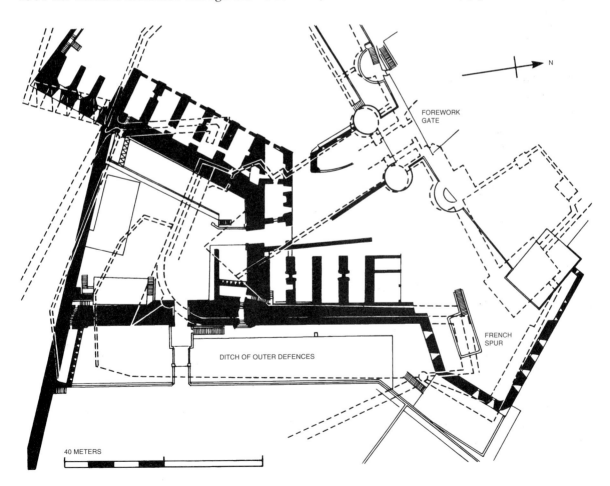

N

FOREWORK GATE

FRENCH SPUR

DITCH OF OUTER DEFENCES

40 METERS

James Stewart created a disturbance that left some of the clergy with bloody heads. During the same visit Mary was lucky to escape with her life when a candle set fire to her bed-hangings while she was asleep. Some observers recalled a prophecy that a queen would be killed by fire in the castle.

It was clearly important that the queen should remarry after a decent interval had elapsed since the death of her first husband, so that she could produce an heir to the kingdom. It seems it was at Stirling Castle that she became infatuated with her kinsman Henry Lord Darnley, who had already been considered as one of a number of possible candidates. He was the elder son of the Earl of Lennox and Margaret Douglas, whose maternal grandmother was thus Queen Margaret Tudor, Mary's own grandmother. Darnley fell ill with measles while at Stirling Castle in April 1565, and the queen took it upon herself to nurse him through it, with consequences that any modern romantic novelist would have predicted as inevitable. The nobility of the kingdom were summoned to Stirling to ratify the queen's decision to marry him, and the marriage took place on 29 July in the private chapel at Holyrood.

The child of this marriage, the future James VI, was born in Edinburgh Castle on 19 June 1566. But if the prestige of Edinburgh Castle made it the most appropriate place for Mary to give birth to Scotland's next king, it was Stirling that was still the natural choice for the royal nursery, and it was not long before he was sent off there to be placed in the care of the Erskine family. It may have been partly in recognition of the importance of his new role that the head of the Erskine family, John Earl of Mar, had his post as captain of the castle made hereditary in July of that year (49). Plans for the baptism of the infant prince in the Chapel Royal there were soon being made, though Mary and her husband were already hopelessly estranged as a result of Darnley's unpredictable behaviour. Her consort was chiefly prominent through his general absence from the festivities, despite being resident within the castle.

The most recent royal occasion to have been celebrated within the Stirling Chapel Royal had been Mary's own coronation. But if that had been a somewhat drab and parsimonious affair, Prince James's baptism was to be the occasion for a spectacle that can have been rivalled by few events elsewhere, even if the queen had to borrow £12,000 from the merchants of Edinburgh to pay for it. Mary probably saw the festivities as a joyful event that would help to heal the rifts that still existed between her magnates, and they were all provided with new costumes of a splendour that was even greater than they might have dared to expect. But, above all, Mary was determined to show Renaissance Europe that a Scottish queen – who was also queen dowager of France – could display herself in as glorious a light as any other European monarch. To achieve this end, it is likely that many of the sequence of themes which were stage-managed with infinite care as the celebrations followed their course were inspired by the *magnificences* that Mary had witnessed when resident in France, and for which France was justly renowned.

The baptism itself took place on 17 December 1566 with full Catholic ritual, the only omission being the spitting into the mouth of the prince by the officiating priest, which the queen prohibited. James was carried from his lodgings to the chapel by the Comte de Brienne, who represented Charles IX of France, where he was met by the Archbishop of St Andrews and the other leaders of the Church. The centrepiece of the service was the font, a magnificent work of art in gold that had been sent by the prince's godmother, Queen Elizabeth of England. Elizabeth was not, of course, present herself, but she was represented by the Duke of Bedford, and the child was held on her behalf by the Countess of Argyll. The only slightly sour note to be struck was that most of the Protestant nobles chose to stay outside the chapel rather than take place in the solemnities. After the service there was dinner in the adjacent great hall, followed by two hours of dancing, music-making and revelry.

On the day after there were formal audiences with ambassadors and hunting, and on the third day, 19 December, there was a dinner at which the main element was an Arthurian round table. The food was served from a moving stage pulled by satyrs, though unfortunately the tails of the satyrs were seen by the English as a joke at their expense, since it was a common Scottish jibe that the English had tails. It also seems that at one point the stage bearing the food collapsed, though none of this was allowed to spoil the general good-humour, which was fostered by delightful music provided by maidens playing upon a wide range of instruments. Later that evening the baby was invested as Prince of Scotland, with all of the titles that went with that, including the dukedom of Rothesay and the earldoms of Carrick, Kyle and Cunningham. The high point of the whole three-day celebrations was the allegorical siege of an enchanted fort that had been constructed on the open ground in front of the castle. Mary watched this event from a specially constructed stand, along with the ambassadors of France, England and Savoy, whose rulers were the prince's godparents, and the climax was a magnificent display of fireworks and artillery.

Unfortunately, if Mary had hoped the baptismal celebrations would open the dawn of a more glorious phase of her reign, she had done little else to achieve this, and it was not to happen. Subsequent events have clouded the last months of her personal rule, but it later came to be believed that Mary may even have been involved in planning the death of her husband while staying at Craigmillar Castle a few weeks before going to Stirling for the baptism. Although on balance it seems unlikely that she would have been personally implicated, it is certainly the case that Darnley died in unexplained circumstances at the Kirk o' Field in Edinburgh

49 *The first Earl of Mar (by permission, the Earl of Mar).*

on 9 February 1567, and from then events moved fast towards her enforced abdication.

Her growing sense of insecurity both on her own account and that of her son, who was a natural target for any disaffected nobles, is suggested by the way that she commanded James should be brought to her at Holyrood in February. This was perhaps so that she could personally watch over his safety, though there may also have been more mundane reasons because on a visit to him at Stirling the previous month she had complained about the dampness of his lodging and the risk that he might develop rheumatism. However, shortly afterwards he was returned to Stirling under the superintendence of the Earls of Huntly and Argyll, where he was once again under the care of the Earl of Mar; the queen, who seems to have been a devoted mother by the standards of the age, found the opportunity to pay a visit to the prince there on 21–2 April. By that time, however, the Earl of Bothwell had already established his hold over the queen and, after abducting her on her return from Stirling, they were married at Holyrood in May, irreversibly alienating many of her nobility.

Following a futile attempt to regain the support of a sufficient body of magnates, Mary surrendered herself at Carberry on 15 June 1567 and was taken to the island castle of Loch Leven. There she was forced to abdicate on 24 July. Prince James, who was thirteen months old, was crowned as James VI on 29 July in the parish church of the Holy Rude at Stirling (see **92**). The crowning and anointing were carried out by Bishop Adam Bothwell of Orkney, and the oath was taken on the new king's behalf by the Earl of Morton and Lord Home. The sermon was preached by John Knox, who apparently objected to certain parts of the ceremony.

James VI

Stirling Castle was to be the young James VI's main place of residence throughout the earlier years of his life and reign (**50**). His chief mentor there from the age of four was the strict disciplinarian George Buchanan, a fine scholar and poet who had been principal of St Leonard's College in St Andrews. James appears to have been an able pupil but it is likely he was lonely and isolated, despite having school fellows who included the young second Earl of Mar. For all his undoubted academic integrity, Buchanan had been a strong opponent of Queen Mary, and did much to poison the young king's mind against his mother. This, together with constant reminders that his father had been murdered by allies of his mother, must have given James a pathetically ambivalent view of his own parents. He must also have been aware that his place of residence was periodically a prison for some of those who were regarded as having played a part in the death of his father. Maitland of Lethington was held there at the end of 1569, and two years later the aged Archbishop John

50 *James VI (by permission, Scottish National Portrait Gallery).*

Hamilton of St Andrews was briefly imprisoned before being hanged at the Market Cross.

During his minority, until he reached the age of twelve, the country was ruled by a succession of regents: the Earls of Moray, Lennox, Mar and Morton. As previous royal minorities had shown, few regents were able to rise above the factions which tended to divide the nobility at such periods, and the place where the king was held would always be a prime focus for those who wished to seize power. This was especially the case during the years when Mary's supporters still had hopes that she might be reinstated. In 1571, after a parliament had been called at Stirling in the young king's name, the leader of the queen's party, Sir William Kirkcaldy of Grange, instigated an attack on the castle on the night of 3 September in the hope of taking prisoner those who had been at the parliament. Although the attack started well, it proved impossible to get the prisoners away, and in its course the regent Lennox, James's grandfather, was killed.

The king assumed nominal control of the kingdom shortly before reaching the age of twelve in 1578, after the deeply unpopular Regent Morton had been constrained to resign. Morton's resignation was engineered when the Earls of Atholl and Argyll persuaded the king to summon a convention of nobles to Stirling on 4 March to judge between themselves and the regent. However, Morton was not to give up so easily. He was possibly the guiding spirit behind a serious affray at the castle on 27 April between the Master of Erskine, who was then guardian of both the king and castle, and his nephew, the young Earl of Mar. The Earl of Mar's own aim was perhaps to press his claim to be guardian of the king's person, in which he was successful, but the Earl of Morton was quick to take advantage of the situation. Although he was supposed to have been in voluntary retirement at Loch Leven Castle, enjoying the consolations of philosophy and gardening, it was not long before he was him-

51 *Huntingtower Castle.*

self at Stirling and in control of both the king and the Earl of Mar, though he was wise enough not to attempt formally to revive his regency. To reinforce his position Morton arranged that the parliament that was to have been held at Edinburgh on 10 July was instead held in the great hall at Stirling on 15 July, where it was opened by the king himself.

Morton's ascendancy over the king began to be eclipsed when a nephew of regent Lennox, Esmé Stewart, the Seigneur d'Aubigny, arrived from France in September 1579. James became infatuated with his new-found cousin, possibly subconsciously treating him as the father he had never known; honours and favours were showered on him, including the dukedom of Lennox. Inevitably this created jealousies in a court where personal success depended on the king's favour. There were fears for the king's person in 1580, when it was rumoured that Esmé Stewart intended to take the king from Stirling to Dumbarton on 10 April, and a strong guard was placed around the king at Stirling by the Earl of Mar. Nothing came of this feared abduction, and the whole thing could have been a figment of Mar's imagination; but it is symptomatic of the degree of polarization of the factions that were developing within the kingdom. Through all of this, Morton progressively fell out of favour and was eventually arrested on 31 December 1580, being executed the following year.

If the fears of a royal abduction came to nothing in 1580, the fact that this was a real risk was to be seen most clearly in the so-called Ruthven Raid of 22 August 1582. A group of those nobles who were particularly alienated by the king's dependence on Esmé Stewart, led by the Earls of Gowrie and Mar, seized the king when at Perth and took him to Gowrie's castle at Huntingtower on the outskirts of the city, which was then known as the House of Ruthven (51). With the king in their control, Esmé Stewart was persuaded that he had no option other than to return to France. The king himself was taken to Stirling, remaining under the control of Gowrie and his confeder-ates for the next ten months. He eventually escaped from the conspirators in June 1583, and at first showed leniency towards them. But on 17 April 1584 the Earls of Mar and Angus, together with the Lords John and Claud Hamilton, seized Stirling Castle, only surren-dering it when the king unexpectedly appeared before it with an army he had raised in Edinburgh. The rebels fled, taking refuge in England. Gowrie was tried for his supposed part in planning the siege, however, and was executed in front of the castle on 4 May.

The king suffered another siege at the castle in the following year, when Queen Elizabeth of England permitted the exiled Earls of Mar and Angus to return to Scotland. After a rapid march across the south of the country they forced an entry into the town of Stirling, and planted their banners immediately in front of the spur that had been built by Mary of Guise. The castle was inadequately provisioned at the time, showing that the attack had come as a complete surprise, and the king had little alter-native but to surrender. His attackers professed their unwavering loyalty, asking only that they should be reinstated to their former honours, and that the Earl of Arran, whom they saw as their particular enemy, should be banished. It casts an illuminating sidelight on the politics of the period that the magnates saw no inconsis-tency in seizing the king in pursuit of their personal aims, while still protesting their loy-alty. Faced with such a succession of startlingly forceful expressions of 'loyalty' before he had reached the age of twenty, it is hardly surpris-ing that the king should have tended to react somewhat nervously to unexpected events in later years.

The castle in the time of James VI

In all this time the castle seems to have been falling into a state of some decay, which is cata-logued in an estimate for necessary works of 7 May 1583 among the accounts of the masters of works. The great hall was said to be letting water in, and the timbers of its roof were being damaged because the roofing itself was defec-tive. The roofs of the forework towers were apparently uncovered, while the roof of the west range of the palace was in a state of col-lapse. The Chapel Royal was leaking so much that the king could not remain in it when it rained; a problem seems to have been that its roof had been built out of true, and many of the rafters had been damaged as a result.

The report suggested a number of radical solutions. While recognizing that the palace was the most pleasant and substantial building in the castle, it was pointed out that it was not well planned to enjoy the glorious views that could be had from the castle (see 3). It was therefore suggested that its ruined west range should be dismantled, the materials being reused to build a kennel in the nether bailey. On its site a new lodging was to be built for the king, with a gallery and terrace, and provision was to be made for the queen and her ladies to pass directly from her lodging into a loft in the chapel, presumably by way of the King's Old Building. It was further suggested that the chapel itself should be rebuilt closer to the north curtain-wall, presumably where the present building now stands, so that the inner close of the castle 'will stand neirby upone sqware in all partis'. It was ingenuously stated that all of these 'workis wilbe large expens', and it is con-sequently very doubtful if much was done.

The picture of neglect and decay within the castle suggested by this report is borne out by an inventory drawn up on 30 November 1585, which suggests the king was surrounded by something well short of luxury. The great hall had just a dining-table, a bench, a dais, a ladder and a chest for clothing, though presumably this great space was used relatively rarely and additional furniture was brought in when needed. The inventory for the king's lodging is interesting for showing what furniture was to be found there, and for giving the sequence of rooms, which were named as his outer hall, his own hall and his chamber. The first room in the sequence had no more than a shelved stand and a wooden chandelier. The next room had five pieces of tapestry, a red damask canopy with gold fringes, a cupboard and a wooden chandelier. The bedchamber was the most richly furnished. It had a bed of red-embroidered velvet fringed with gold, and with appropriately rich hangings and covers; there were also a canopy of cloth of gold, seven pieces of tapestry, two tables with a Turkey carpet on the larger of the two, and a coffer within which was the spear for the king's standard.

Yet the picture is not all gloom, and some essential repairs were certainly made in the castle over these years. John Stewart, the constable of the castle, had submitted an account for works costing £18 10s.4d. on 26 June 1576, and there must have been other works of which no record survives. We know that a stretch of the north curtain-wall between the upper part of the castle and the nether bailey had collapsed, for example, and it seems very likely that the section of this which incorporates a spur-shaped projection was rebuilt in the later sixteenth century. The most glaring loss from the accounts is that for the rebuilding of the Chapel Royal, though we know a little of what was done from other sources.

The reason for rebuilding the chapel was the baptism of the first son of James VI, and this was unquestionably the most splendid event to take place within the castle during his personal reign. James had married Anne of Denmark on 20 August 1589, and Prince Henry was born within the castle on 19 February 1594. The twenty-seven-year-old king at last had an heir and the whole country, with the prospect of greater security ahead, was ready to rejoice. The report of 1583 had made it clear that the old chapel was no longer fit to house a major ceremony. In view of this, the decision was taken to rebuild it, following the recommendation of the report that it should be set further back towards the north curtain-wall in order to give the inner close the more regular shape that had probably been first considered by James IV about a century before. It was said that £100,000 Scots was voted for the rebuilding, and the work must have been carried out a breakneck rate, because the new chapel was ready for the baptism by 30 August. Various lesser works were also carried out to bring the castle as a whole into a state that would pass muster, in a flurry of activity that cost £1053 6s.10d. (This account is incidentally interesting for showing that the rooms in the king's lodging were by then referred to as the hall, the chamber of presence and the bedchamber.)

The new chapel is a large but relatively simple rectangular structure of 34.3 by 11.35m (112 by 37ft). The main architectural emphasis is concentrated on the façade towards the close, which has an arched central doorway framed within a triumphal arch motif, consisting of pairs of columns resting on plinths and carrying an entablature (52). Along the walls on each side of this doorway are three windows of Italianate design, each with a semicircular arch framing a pair of round-headed openings; between the heads of the openings are traces of decoration which later accounts suggest included a crown and the royal monogram. There is a similar but larger window in the east wall, with a second doorway in the west wall, and there was possibly a third one in the north wall. The west end of the chapel is connected to the King's Old Building, with a small chamber above a transe, the chamber perhaps serving as a vestibule to a royal loft for the queen within the chapel. On the evidence of a break in the external base course, there may also have been an intention to build a vestry on the north side of the chapel though we have no evidence that this was ever built. Also on the north side was a cross-wall going back to the curtain-wall, evidently to define an open corridor leading to the south-western section of the north curtain. At the south-east corner of the chapel there seems to have been an intention to build a

52 *The Chapel Royal, from the inner close.*

small link building to the hall, though this was only added later.

Internally, the combined evidence of a later scheme of painted decoration and of eighteenth-century survey drawings suggests that the ceiling was of polygonal profile, which could have been left either as open timbers or, more probably, boarded or plastered over (see 54). According to Robert Johnstone, a contemporary historian, the ceiling was decorated in gold, and the walls hung with pictures, sculptures and other carvings for the occasion of the baptism. Little is known of the furnishings, though a badly damaged pulpit still at the castle is traditionally said to have been made for the chapel.

The baptism itself was organized by Sir Patrick Leslie as Master of Ceremonies, together with the master of works, William Fowler. Two days of festivities preceded the service, during which there were chivalric sports, while several gentlemen of the court disported themselves in female dress as Amazons. At the baptism the prince was carried to the chapel by Queen Elizabeth of England's representative, the Earl of Sussex. During the service the king was seated in the north-east corner of the chapel, flanked by the ambassadors of France, England, Brunswick, the Low Countries, Denmark and Magdeburg. The sermon was preached by Patrick Galloway, and the baptism was performed by Bishop Cunningham of Aberdeen, who afterwards delivered an oration in Latin from the pulpit to the – doubtlessly delighted – ambassadors. After the ceremony the prince was invested with the titles of the heir to the throne, and a number of knights were dubbed.

The banquet in the great hall which followed was a wonderful spectacle. Food was brought in on a chariot drawn by a richly attired Moor. This was followed by a ship 5.5m (18ft) long and 12m(40ft) high, which floated on an artificial sea and carried a variety of fish (53).

53 *A sketch showing how the celebrations in the great hall for the baptism of Prince Henry in 1594 may have appeared (David Pollock).*

Volleys were fired from its thirty-six brass guns, to the consternation of beholders. All of this was followed by a concert lasting until after midnight. To make the hall more suitable for the celebrations there may have been some structural alterations, because there are traces of an inserted doorway near the centre of the wall towards the inner close which has mouldings of the type that might be expected around this period.

CHAPTER FOUR

The palace becomes a fortress

The homecoming of James VI

Queen Elizabeth I of England died on 24 March 1603. In accordance with the wishes that she had at last been prevailed upon to express, James VI was immediately declared James I of England by the English privy council. The crowns of the two kingdoms were thus united in his person, though there was as yet no question of a union of the kingdoms themselves. On going to England James declared that Scotland would retain its place in his affections, and that he and his successors would make frequent 'homecomings' to their northern kingdom. As it happened, however, James was only ever in Scotland again between 13 May and 4 August 1617, while Charles I only visited briefly around the time of his Scottish coronation in June 1633, and again between 14 August and 17 November 1641 after war had broken out between the king and his English parliament.

The last period of Scottish residence by a king of the Stewart dynasty was to be between 23 June 1650 and 5 August 1651, when Charles II was attempting to rally support against Cromwell, and during which period he was crowned as king of Scotland at Scone on 1 January 1651. But his experiences in Scotland, when he was coerced into signing the Covenants calling for a Presbyterian system of Church government, as well as being lectured on the duties of a godly king, filled him with little wish to return there after his restoration to the English

throne in 1660. Although he was persuaded to create a fitting Scottish palace at Holyrood in the 1670s, he had no intention of being drawn into more than a basic minimum of expenditure on the other royal residences, and his reign was thus one of the turning-points in Stirling Castle's history. Until that time it had functioned both as a fortress and as a royal residence, with the emphasis shifting between the two as circumstances required. But from the later seventeenth century onwards it was the former function that almost entirely dictated what was done.

However, that lies in the future, and we must now return to consider the castle's last years of active use as a royal residence. More than £13,000 was spent on it in preparation for James VI's visit in 1617, most of the work being carried out to the directions of the mason William Rhynd and evidently being of a fairly mundane nature. James made two brief stays at the castle in July, and on the 19th he heard a learned discourse by the principal and regents of Edinburgh University within the chapel. The visit may have prompted a slightly more regular approach to basic maintenance, though it is doubtful if this kept pace with accelerating decay.

The homecoming of Charles I

The succession of Charles I in 1625 and the expectation of a visit to Scotland for his coronation led to further repairs. In the year of his

54 *The interior of the Chapel Royal before recent restoration, showing the decoration added by Valentine Jenkin for the 'homecoming' of Charles I in 1633.*

succession William Wallace, the royal master mason, was enlivening the skyline of the castle with carvings of heraldic beasts along the ridge of the hall, and the gardener William Watts was sent from England to look into the state of the gardens at the Scottish residences. Repairs were also carried out to the roofs of the hall and chapel, but it was said that extensive work was needed on the west range of the palace (see **37**), as well as to the roof of the king's closets on the opposite side of the Lion's Den. Much of this sounds suspiciously like what had already been urged as necessary in 1583, though by now it had to be said that parts of the foundations of the west range had fallen over the cliff. As with a great deal that was

done, we get the impression that it was the bare minimum on each occasion, and that it was seldom enough.

As it happened, Charles felt unable to leave England for several years, though activity on the palaces intensified in 1628–9 on the evidence of the surviving accounts of the masters of works. The painter Valentine Jenkin, together with his assistants Andrew Home and John Binning, had already been at the castle in 1617, but the first two of those were to be even more active from 1628. Among other things, they gilded the royal arms over the gateway. At the same time the hall was painted white above the string course and blue below it, while the string course itself and the fireplaces were painted with simulated marbling. Within the royal lodgings they decorated the upper walls of the queen's bedchamber above the hangings with 'antikis' to conform with those on the ceiling; this was presumably some sort of Classical decoration that would reflect the design of the ceiling. In the king's lodging it was particularly stressed that the doorways and fireplaces were to be marbled. Such references remind us that stonework was not usually left unpainted, and that colour schemes could be very rich by modern standards. Even the external stonework was usually rendered or lime-washed, and recent removal of the blocking of the hall windows has revealed extensive traces of limewash there.

It is interesting to note that by this date the sequence of rooms in the lodgings was being listed as the guard hall, the great chamber and the bedchamber. However, the names could clearly vary because, while one of the masters of works' accounts for 1613–14 had referred to them as hall, chamber of presence and bed-chamber, by the early eighteenth century the two outer rooms were to be named as guard hall and presence chamber. But, whatever names were used, the functions of the sequence remained essentially the same. The outer or guard hall was still the largest and most public room of the sequence, and it was there that the royal guard was posted to ensure that only those who had rights of access went further into the lodging. The great chamber or presence chamber was the room where the king, or queen, would grant audiences, and their presence would be denoted by a cloth of estate even when they were not there in person; they might also eat in this room with honoured guests or with the more favoured members of their household. The bedchamber was still both a state bedroom and a more intimate living-room, and access there was even more limited.

Among the grandest schemes instigated at this time was that for the chapel, though the Scottish Chapel Royal was by now regarded as being the nave of the old abbey church of Holyrood near Edinburgh, and it was there that Charles's coronation was to be carried out. Parts of the decorative scheme executed by Jenkin and his assistant on the walls and ceiling of the chapel walls at Stirling were rediscovered in the 1930s and were subse-quently restored (54). Running around the interior of the chapel, below the wall-head, is a painted Classical entablature. Its frieze is richly embellished with fruit and with strapwork-decorated panels bearing the letters CIR (the C and R are abbreviations for Carolus Rex, meaning King Charles, though it is not clear if the I is a Roman numeral referring to Charles as first of that name, or if it was the initial of his father, James VI, who had built the chapel). Also on the frieze are depicted the Honours of Scotland used at the coronation: the sword, sceptre and crown. In the upper part of the west wall is a painted window to reflect the real window in the east gable, and above it is the crown and crest of Scotland. The 'jeistis' of the ceiling (presumably meaning the ribs) were to have flowers on a blue ground decorated with 'antikis' which, as in the queen's lodging, would have been some form of Classical deco-ration. The predominant colour throughout was 'blew gray'.

The gardens both within and below the castle were evidently extensively modified in 1628–9. Robert Norrie and James Rhynd were making balusters for the terrace overlooking the bowl-ing green, in front of the western section of the forework; a fragment of this still survives against the stump of the wall belonging to the outworks of around 1559. The orchard and garden were also worked on, the garden referred to here probably being that in the valley to the west of the castle, of which the earth-works, known as the King's Knot, survive (55). The most prominent feature of these is the elab-orately modelled earthwork at the southern end of the garden area, the earthwork that some later writers were to interpret as the setting for King Arthur's round table. Within a square raised walk is a complex three-tiered octagonal mound, and the whole design is intersected by a cross-pattern of walks. To the north of this is a more shallowly modelled earthwork, with a

55 *The King's Knot, the gardens in the valley to the the south-west of the castle.*

rectangle framing an oval at the centre of the larger rectangle, and again there is a cross-pattern of paths. From what we know of such gardens in England, it is likely that the more complex portion would have had low hedges to further define its lines, with specimen shrubs at the main points. The other section probably also had its raised beds defined by hedges, but within that framework there could have been knot-patterns of box hedging.

Further minor works were carried out immediately before the king's coronation visit in 1633, including the construction of new stabling. Considering all the preparations that were made at Stirling and elsewhere in his realm, it is a pity that, when his visit finally took place, the king succeeded in alienating much of his natural support through his high-handed behaviour and lack of understanding of the Scottish way of doing things. Particularly obnoxious were his policies for the Church, for which he wished to introduce services following English practices more closely in their form and ritual, and which was to be governed by a strengthened episcopate. This eventually led to the signing of the National Covenant in February 1638, which called for the restoration of a Presbyterian system of Church organization. Events were now in train for open warfare in Scotland, and by March 1639 the king was marching north at the head of an ill-prepared army. Peace of a sort was achieved in 1641, but by the following year he was also at war with the English parliamentary party, a war which culminated in his own defeat, and ultimately in his execution on 30 January 1649.

The castle in the time of Charles II and James VII

Despite their distaste for many of Charles I's policies, most Scots were deeply shocked at his execution by the English, and his son was immediately declared king in Scotland as Charles II. In doing this they antagonized their previous allies, Oliver Cromwell and the English Parliamentarians. The arrival of their new king in Scotland in June 1650 made Cromwell turn his attention north of the border, though he was himself to return to England after the capture of Perth on 3 August. The taking of Stirling Castle was thus left to Lieutenant-General George Monk. After he had forced the town to surrender, on 7 August Monk began to lay siege to the castle itself, constructing platforms for his artillery within the churchyard, and possibly also firing from the church tower. The garrison of the castle, consisting of about 300 men under the command of Colonel William Cunningham, returned fire, but by 13 and 14 August Monk was able to bring his mortars and great guns into play with devastating effect, as a result of which the garrison mutinied. Cunningham was forced to negotiate, and was allowed to surrender honourably.

The siege caused considerable damage both to the castle and to the church, and the marks

of shot are still to be seen on the upper south gable of the great hall. By far the greatest loss which resulted from the siege, however, was the eventual destruction of many of Scotland's State records. These had been held in the castle at the time of the siege, and were removed from there to England afterwards; unfortunately some of them were lost at sea when they were being returned to Scotland following the restoration of the monarchy. After the siege the castle was placed in the care of Colonel Reade, who proposed to Cromwell that it should have a garrison of thirteen companies of foot and a regiment of horse.

Following the Restoration, in 1661 the governorship of the castle was once again entrusted to the Earl of Mar. Although Charles II had no intention himself of coming north, during his reign his brother and heir-presumptive, James Duke of Albany and York, was sent at times when his open Catholicism made it unwise for him to remain in England. When in Scotland he also served as his brother's commissioner to the Scottish parliament. Duke James paid a visit to Stirling on 3–4 February 1681, but despite repairs that had been carried out to the palace two years earlier, involving new roofs, floors and the insertion of casement windows, the castle was apparently not in a state that would allow him to stay there. He instead stayed in the town house of the Earl of Argyll (see **97**), though was evidently much impressed by the castle and its setting when conducted around it by the Earl of Mar. In the year of his visit a powder magazine was built to the north of the King's Old Building (**56**), perhaps an indicator that military needs were coming to be seen as more important than those of royal residence.

The later seventeenth century was a time of continuing religious conflict in Scotland, and a number of the prisoners held in the castle were there because of their beliefs. There were several notable Covenanter prisoners in the 1660s and 1670s, including Major-General Robert Montgomery, Sir William Cunningham of

Cunningham and Sir William Muir of Rowallan. The so-called 'Killing Time' of the 1680s, which followed the field preacher Richard Cameron's public renunciation of his allegiance to the king and his heir, was a particularly dark phase in the nation's history, though the government clearly had little alternative to suppressing what, on any assessment, was open rebellion.

Also in the 1680s concern was expressed about the security of the crossing of the Forth at Stirling, and Lord Dartmouth was commissioned to investigate in October 1684. In the following year, perhaps as a result of the abortive rising led by the Earl of Argyll in March, designs were drawn up by Major Martin Beckman for an elaborate artillery fortification at the end of the bridge closest to the castle. This fort would have covered about 8ha (20 acres), and by 2 May a governor and captain were even being appointed for it, though it was never to be built, and attention soon shifted back to the castle itself. From at least 1685 Stirling Castle had become an official army establishment, with the Earl of Mar being formally appointed as the captain of its garrison on 30 March 1685; Captain Archibald Stewart was appointed its lieutenant and John Erskine its ensign.

The start of the Jacobite threat

The Duke of Albany and York succeeded his brother as James VII of Scotland and II of England in February 1685. One of his cherished aims was to restore Catholicism to his two kingdoms, and he immediately set about

56 The powder magazine to the north of the King's Old Building, on the site of that built in 1681.

trying to remove the penalties that had been introduced against Catholic worship, offering at the same time the prospect of religious liberty so long as there was no question of disloyalty. Needless to say, however, religious liberty was among the last things that the extremists on either side were looking for. But it was events in England, and in particular moves that were seen as threatening the interests of the Church of England, that led to James VII's premature flight to France on 11 December 1688. In the following year his daughter Mary and her husband, William Prince of Orange, who was also a grandson of Charles I, were invited to take up the two crowns. This offer was made by an English convention held on 13 February, and by a Scottish convention which met on 14 March.

The deposed direct line of the Stewarts, however, was to remain an active focus of discontent for over half a century, and much of what was done to Stirling Castle over those years was in response to that threat. James VII himself lived until 1701, but after his death his claims to the throne were continued first by his son James, the 'Old Pretender', who died in 1766, and then by his grandson Charles, the 'Young Pretender', popularly known as Bonnie Prince Charlie, who died in 1788. Although the threat largely passed with the failure of the rising of 1745–6 and the defeat at Culloden, it was only the death in 1807 of Charles's brother, Henry Cardinal York, that saw the formal end of the claims of the main branch of the Stewart dynasty.

The existence of a rival line naturally provided a series of figureheads both for those who sincerely believed that James and his successors should be reinstated, and for those who saw themselves as having been either disadvantaged or slighted by the monarchs who replaced them. Episcopalians – those who wished to see the Scottish Church governed by bishops – tended to be particularly associated with the cause, since William and Mary abolished bishops within the established Church, reintroducing a system of Presbyterian organization. Their adherence was in spite of the fact that James and his successors were Catholic. Those who supported the claims of the deposed line came to be known as Jacobites, since the Latin version of the name James is Jacobus. The earliest rebellion in his name took place as soon as the convention of 14 March 1689 was called, and was led by John Graham of Claverhouse, Viscount Dundee, though Dundee's death at the battle of Killiecrankie in July brought that rising to an end. The rebellion demonstrated the need for bringing Scotland's main castles into line with modern requirements, and it was as a result of a report submitted in 1689 that improvements were made to the perimeter defences at Stirling.

To create a single point of entry to the castle, a small postern gate in the outer wall of the nether bailey, for which a new door had only been provided in the previous year, was blocked (57). To provide better emplacements for cannon, the vaults of the kitchens along the north-east curtain-wall were removed, and the kitchens themselves infilled to create a firm base for an artillery battery overlooking Gowan Hill (see 29). At the same time another battery was formed near the bowling green, presumably to the south of the section of the forework overlooked by the palace. It was also very likely as part of this campaign that the Elphinstone Tower was cut down, its vaults infilled, and an artillery battery formed at the same level as the battery above the kitchens; this had certainly been done by the time that Slezer drew the castle in the last decades of the century (see 22). Much of the masonry work involved in these operations was the responsibility of Tobias and Thomas Bauchop.

Between 1699 and 1703 the Bauchops went on to carry out extensive work on the top floor of the palace block, where the governor of the castle now had his apartment, and several fireplaces and doorways still date from this

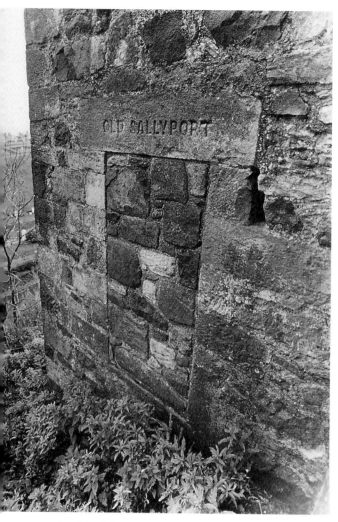

57 The blocked postern gate in the nether bailey.

period. A new external stair was also built up to the top floor, though the walls and porch which now enclose it are not shown on drawings before 1719, and may therefore represent an improvement made between 1708 and 1714, when various other works were being carried out (58).

Queen Mary died in 1694 and King William in 1702; they were succeeded by Queen Anne, the second daughter of James VII, but over the following years many Scots were to feel themselves increasingly alienated by events happening in the southern kingdom. By the time she came to the throne Anne's only surviving child had already died and, to ensure the succession, the English parliament decided that the children of Sophia, Electress of Hanover, should be recognized as next in line. Sophia was a granddaughter of James VI by his daughter Queen Elizabeth of Bohemia, and she was undoubtedly the natural successor since the deposition of James VII and II if James's own heirs were lawfully barred from the succession. But considerable numbers of Scotland's leaders felt they had not been properly consulted in this decision, and saw it as symptomatic of the way their views were coming to be disregarded. An even greater point of tension for many was the decision that the parliaments of the two kingdoms should be united, and thus in effect the two kingdoms brought together into one. The last session of the Scottish parliament was closed on 28 April 1707, and the formal Treaty of Union came into effect on 1 May.

By this stage Britain had been at war with France for some years, and King Louis XIV of France, who regarded himself as the champion of the Catholic cause, saw in the latest developments the opportunity to place the Old Pretender on his father's throne by fostering a rising in Scotland. He furnished James with a squadron of ships together with a force of 6000 soldiers, which reached the Firth of Forth on 23 March 1708. The whole project was misjudged and with hindsight we can see that it was easily repelled; but it caused the greatest consternation at Westminster, and it was decided that the major Scottish castles should again be immediately strengthened. It was because of this that the last major changes were made to the defences of Stirling Castle.

The outer defences

Orders for the strengthening of Stirling and Edinburgh Castles and of Fort William were issued on 1 April 1708, and by 25 June Captain Thedore Dury, the military engineer for Scotland, had prepared designs costed for

Stirling at £6440 13s.6d. sterling. Dury proposed to leave the outer defences much as they were, but to add a triangular outer enclosure in front of them where the esplanade now stands, with a gate at its southern apex (**59**). To the south-west of this he proposed to build an outer wall along the edge of the castle rock, with embrasures at its east end to give covering fire along the flank on that side. A start was made on constructing the south side of the main enclosure wall, a length of which is still to be seen (**60** and see **67**). It was apparently built by the mason Thomas Bauchop, whom we have already encountered, together with another mason named as James Watson.

Essential works were also planned and started on several of the buildings within the castle, including repairs to the hall and the roof of the chapel. However, the governor of the castle, the sixth Earl of Mar (see **73**), had

58 The stair to the governor's apartment on the top floor of the palace and the porch to the palace.

earlier expressed concern at the condition of the castle's buildings, and seems to have seen these new works as affording an excuse for more grandiose building operations. It may be added that he was himself an amateur architect of considerable skill who took a close interest in the whole operation. In consequence, work inside the castle was halted and a drawing was prepared which showed far-reaching changes to the buildings around the inner close (**61**). A link building was proposed between the palace and the King's Old Building, containing a spacious kitchen, and a grand stair up to the governor's apartment. A new entrance was to be provided into the main floor of the palace through the hall of the king's lodging. The great hall was to be subdivided, with a banqueting

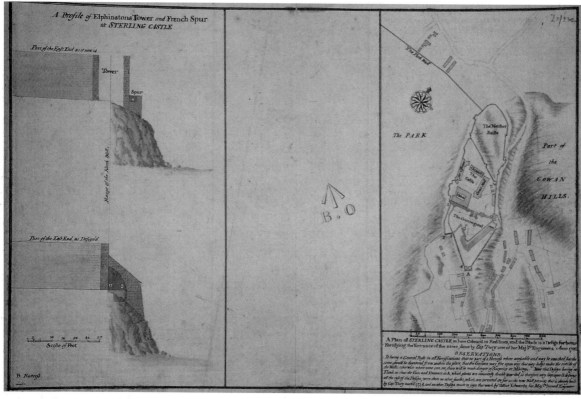

59 A plan showing Dury's proposal for the outer defences (Crown copyright, National Library of Scotland, B.O. Z2/23).
60 The outer defences from the south.

61 A plan of 1709–10 showing proposals for remodelling the buildings around the inner close (Crown copyright, National Library of Scotland, B.O. Z2/17).

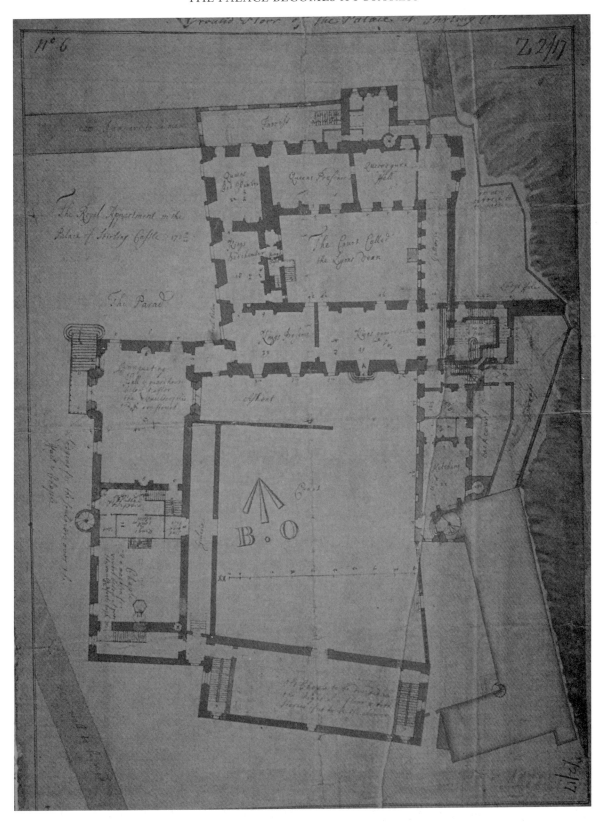

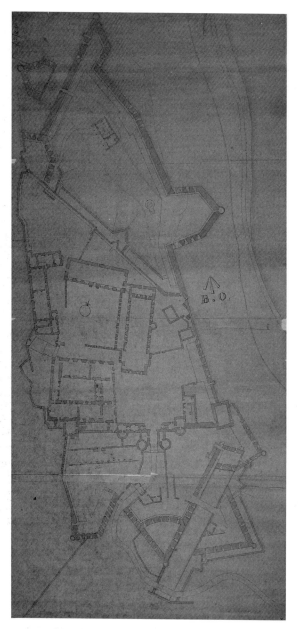

have floors and staircases inserted to allow it to be used as an armoury.

It is difficult to be certain how far these designs were carried through, but it is doubtful if very much was done because a heated discussion was now opened on the whole of Dury's proposals for the defences. Captain Obryan had been sent up from London to report on Dury's activities, and he was evidently shocked by what he saw, stating that the new work left 'all the rest of the castle [apart from the entrance] under no better security than an old rotten wall'. As an alternative to them he proposed a sophisticated system of artillery defences around much of the castle's perimeter (**62**). This scheme would have cost no less than £73,545 4s. sterling. A further report was then prepared on 1 March 1711 by Dury and Obryan's superior officer, Talbot Edwards, following which Dury constructed the outer defences as we now see them, with some undefined involvement by the architect James Smith. From the recommencement of work in April 1711, the masonry was the responsibility of the master mason Gilbert Smith.

The work was largely complete by March 1714. It is perhaps worth mentioning that a report of the 23rd of that month mentioned that five old towers and several decayed walls had been demolished in the process. The towers referred to as being demolished seem likely to have included the two half-round towers flanking the gatehouse of the forework (see **31**). The upper parts of some of the towers of the gatehouse itself were probably also included among the demolitions, since it becomes clear from a series of views engraved in the course of the eighteenth century that the superstructure of the gatehouse was being progressively dismantled (**63**, see **colour plate 5**).

It could not be claimed that the design for the outer defences as eventually built marks a high point in the history of artillery fortification. Yet it does represent a modestly effective solution tailored to a difficult site along a narrow front, in which considerations of economy

62 *A plan showing Captain Obryan's proposals for more extensive strengthening of the outer defences (Crown copyright, National Library of Scotland, B.O. Z2/16b).*

hall at its southern end and a chapel at the northern end, and with a covered gallery running along the courtyard face; barrack rooms for soldiers were to be fitted out above both the new hall and adjacent chapel. The chapel itself, on the north side of the close, was to

63 *An engraving of the castle in 1781, showing the decayed state of the forework gatehouse (S. Middiman and W. Byrne).*

clearly played a significant part. As has been said above, from recent investigations, we now know that the east flank of the great spur that had probably been built in the 1550s was retained, and the line of that face was extended across the whole of the castle rock to create a new forewall (**64**). At its northern end the French Spur was also retained substantially intact, though its open southern flank was walled across, providing positions for cannon at two levels (**65, 66**). At the lower level the cannon were housed in embrasures known as casemates; at the upper level they were set back behind the earth parapets that were formed along all of the new wall-heads with the intention of absorbing any shot striking the

defences at this level. The south flank of the new defences was formed by the much thinner wall that Dury had started in the first phase of operations (**67**). Protective fire was provided along the outer face of this south flank by cannon housed in a triplet of casemates within a low battery (**colour plate 8**).

In front of the new wall and the French Spur the original ditch was deepened, widened and extended, and within the ditch were placed two of the low stone-vaulted firing galleries that are usually known as caponiers, but which

64 (Opposite, above) *The ditch and outer wall of the outer defences.*

65 (Opposite, below) *The French Spur as remodelled in 1708–14.*

66 *The French Spur from above.*

67 *The south wall of the outer defences.*

68 *Inside the surviving caponier in the outer ditch.*

are referred to in the building accounts as 'coffers'. Only one of these caponiers still survives in the outer ditch (68). The new forewall was pierced by a single gateway, which was approached by a bridge across the ditch. At the centre of this bridge was a drawbridge, and eighteenth-century engravings show it was operated from an arch in front of the main entrance, and that it was hung from beams known as gaffes (69).

Within the gateway was a defensive pocket overlooked by higher walls to the north and north-west, in front of which was a second ditch defended by caponiers (70). The inner gate of the defences, which was surmounted by a cannon emplacement that came to be known as the Overport Battery, was given greater architectural enrichment than the outer gate. It was flanked by rusticated Tuscan pilasters, and on its keystone was the crowned monogram of Queen Anne (71). Overlooking three of the outer angles of the new defences were domed pepper-pot-like sentry boxes, referred to in the accounts as 'centinel boxes' (see 67). Additional strength was provided both behind the inner walls and behind the original east wall of the spur by constructing a series of walls at right angles to them, between which ran stone vaults. The casemates formed by these walls and vaults could be used as barrack rooms in times of emergency. Those behind the wall of the old spur (which now house the restaurant) were so high that a timber floor was originally inserted within them, making them two-storeys high; those behind the north-west inner wall, which

69 An engraving of the castle in 1753, showing the drawbridge.

overlooked the bowling green area in front of the forework, were of only a single storey (72). The barrack rooms were equipped with fireplaces at which the soldiers could cook their food, and they were sufficiently complete to be ready for glazing in 1714.

The Jacobite risings of 1715 and 1745

The Earl of Mar, who was governor of the castle during these operations, was also Queen Anne's Scottish Secretary between 1705 and

70 *The guardroom square within the outer defences.*

71 *The royal cypher on the keystone of the inner gate of the outer defences.*

1709, and again in 1713–14 (**73**). But with the accession of George I in 1714 he fell out of favour, and was dismissed both as secretary and as governor of the castle. The earl, who was to earn the unenviable nickname of 'Bobbing John' because of his political fickleness, was not a man to brook such loss of dignity lightly, and rapidly changed his allegiance. On 6 September 1715 he raised the standard of the Old Pretender at Braemar, marking the start of a rising against the new Hanoverian dynasty. After an initial success,

72 *The casemates overlooking the bowling green.*

when Perth was taken for him by Colonel Hay on 14 September, the rising quickly lost impetus, largely as a result of Mar's indecisiveness.

The leader of the Hanoverian forces in Scotland, the Duke of Argyll, seized the initiative, and seeing that control of Stirling Castle was essential for preventing Mar from heading southwards, he established himself there on 17 September. By November Mar was on the move again, and it was necessary for Argyll to lead his main force out of the castle to intercept him. Argyll left the castle under the command of General Wightman, and on 13 November he engaged Mar's army on Sheriffmuir, a little to the east of Dunblane. The battle was something of a fiasco for both sides, though it marked the real end of the rising. By the time the Old Pretender himself arrived at

Peterhead on 22 December it was too late to rally his disenchanted troops, and both he and Mar went into exile.

While in exile, the Earl of Mar found some consolation in cultivating his skills in architectural design, drawing up proposals for a variety of buildings both real and imaginary. One of the most interesting of those proposals was for the palace at Stirling, which he evidently dreamed of making into a fine Baroque residence for the restored Stewart dynasty, with an equally fine apartment for himself on the top floor. The designs were drawn up in April 1724, when the earl was resident in Paris, and in their planning they show points

95

of similarity with the schemes drawn up in 1709–10 (**74, 75**). Externally the palace was to be regularized by the construction of a wide new range on the derelict west side of the building, leaving a remodelled Prince's Tower at the centre of a new south front. All of the original decorative detail on the façades, which must have seemed rather uncouth by this period, was to be suppressed, and square

pavilions with domed roofs were to be raised above the four angles of the building. As in the 1709–10 scheme (see **61**), there was to be a link range between the palace and the King's Old Building, with a handsome staircase up to the governor's apartment on the top floor immediately within the main doorway from that range. Also as in that scheme, the hall was to be drawn into the proposals, with a most imposing salon approached from the king's presence chamber at its southern end. While we may be grateful that James V's palace was not lost to sight below such a remodelling, it would have had an undeniably imposing impact on the castle.

By the time the Earl of Mar was dreaming up his schemes for the palace, a less innovative but more informative series of drawings had

73 *The sixth Earl of Mar. The artillery spur can be seen to his right (by permission, the Earl of Mar).*

74 *The sixth Earl of Mar's proposal for the remodelling of the south front of the palace (Scottish Record Office, RHP 13258/45–49; by permission, the Keeper of the Records of Scotland).*

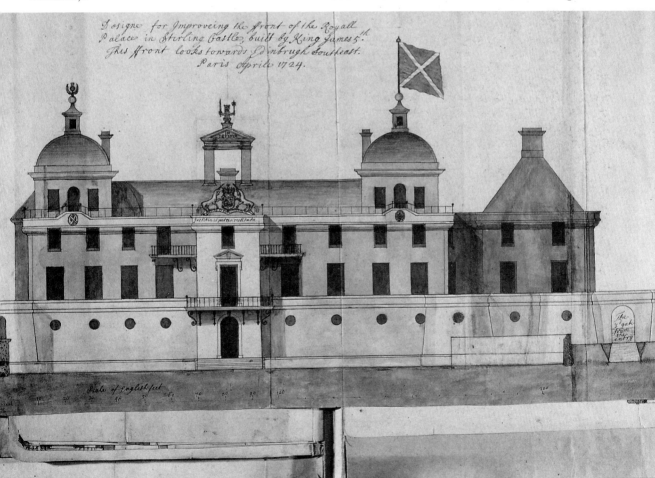

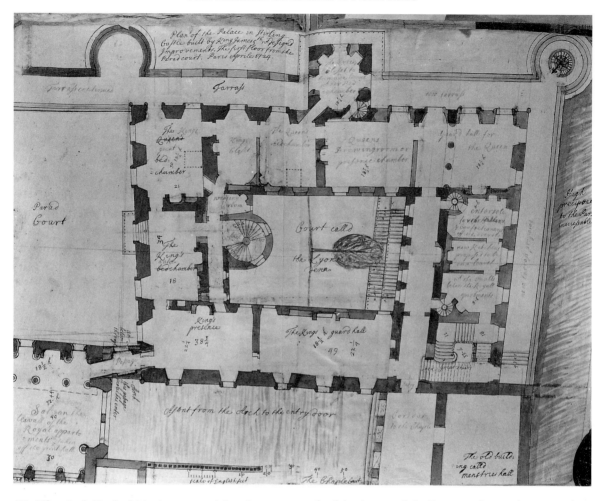

75 *The sixth Earl of Mar's proposal for the planning of the principal floor in the palace (Scottish Record Office, RHP 13258/45–49; by permission, the Keeper of the Records of Scotland).*

been prepared. These were the fruit of an official survey of 1719, and are invaluable for showing us the state of many of the buildings within the castle at that time; indeed, the cross-section of the hall is the most important piece of evidence we have for the hammerbeam roof that still covered it (**76** and see **23**). The 1719 survey is of additional importance for showing us the use of the buildings as the military take-over of them continued, even though at this stage in the castle's history there was little more than a skeleton garrison. In the palace the king's guard hall was a barrack room, but the rest of the grand rooms on the main floor were either empty or used for storage. The upper floor continued to be allocated to the governor and his housekeeper, and he had a stable and a brewhouse in the vaulted undercrofts of the hall. A floor had been inserted within at least part of the hall, though that superb space seems to have been largely unused, as was perhaps also the chapel. The survey also shows that the lean-to corridor along the inner close side of the hall had been walled in, and that it had windows and a central doorway. On the opposite side of the close from the hall the King's Old Building housed the major and the chaplain, as well as a bakehouse and a small infirmary, but much of the rest was divided up for storage. Above the north gate was the brewhouse, while there was a storeroom for the gunner on its top floor.

An almost identical situation is revealed in a second set of drawings of 1741, suggesting that the castle was fast becoming a military as well as a royal backwater. However, the peace that had descended on it was soon to be disturbed. In August 1745 Bonnie Prince Charlie landed in Scotland at the start of another campaign to claim the throne for his father. Having crossed the Forth at a point upstream from the castle, where the government soldiers fled at the sight of him, he marched his army through Stirling on 14 September. Little more than a few token shots were fired at him from the castle. But, having reached as far south as Derby in Midland England by December, he could persuade his generals to advance no further, and the march back to Scotland began.

Despite earlier indecision by Sir John Cope, the leader of the government forces in Scotland, Stirling had become one of the main bases for the government army, and was under the command of the able General Blakeney. Nevertheless, on 6 January 1746 the town of Stirling was surrendered by its magistrates to the rebel army, of which the main contingent was based on the outskirts of the town at St Ninians. The decision was then taken by Prince Charles to lay siege to the castle. His principal siege-works were established on Gowan Hill, immediately to the north-east of the castle, under the direction of the Comte Mirabelle de Gourdon (see 77). This, however, was against the advice of some of his generals, who were by now at loggerheads with one another. Such a position was both uncomfortably close to the castle's grand

76 *One of the sheets of the survey of 1719 showing the hall and King's Old Building (Crown Copyright, National Library of Scotland, B.O. Z2/18b).*

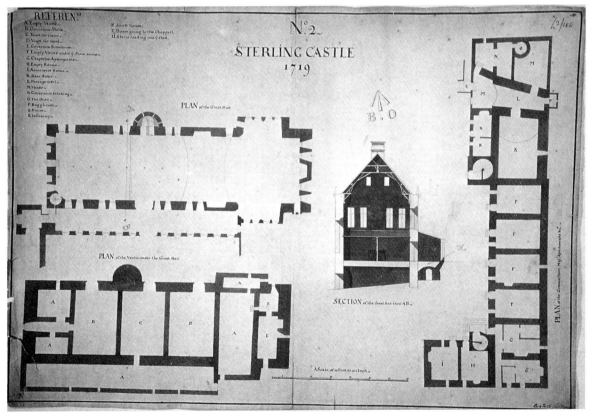

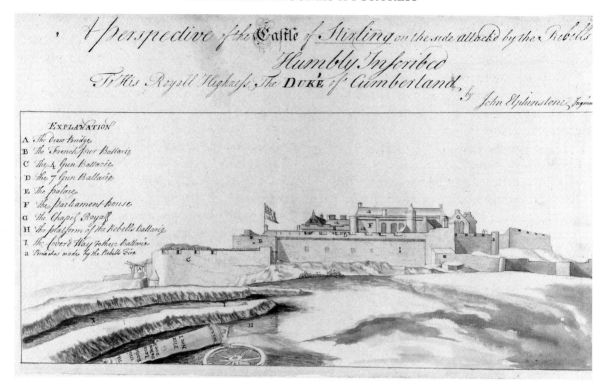

77 *The site of the artillery battery on Gowan Hill in the siege by Bonnie Prince Charlie of 1746 (by Permission, British Library, K. Top L 96 f. 1.1).*

battery, and on terrain that did not lend itself to the construction of defensive earthworks.

Blakeney bided his time until 28 and 29 January, when de Gourdon's only partly finished battery ill-advisedly started playing on the walls of the castle. Blakeney returned fire with his superior armament, destroying de Gourdon's inadequate emplacement within a very short space of time. This brought to an abrupt end the last siege the castle ever suffered. The position of the destroyed Jacobite battery in relation to the castle is graphically portrayed in a drawing made by the engineer John Elphinstone for the Duke of Cumberland (77). As the duke's army approached on 1 February the Jacobites retreated in some disarray, with little alternative to abandoning much of their artillery and powder. The former were spiked to prevent them being used by the government forces, while the powder was blown up, unfortunately destroying St Ninian's church, where it was stored, in the process. When the Jacobite army had been routed at Culloden in April, limited repairs were carried out on many of the Scottish castles, including Stirling.

Later building works in the castle

The architect William Adam, who was master mason to the Board of Ordnance as well as designer of some of the finest country houses erected in Scotland, was involved in the post-1746 repairs, though it is difficult to be certain what his precise contribution was at Stirling. Inevitably, all of the building operations carried out in the castle over the following decades were essentially utilitarian in character, as befitted their military use, though this did not always mean that they were unworthy of their setting. Perhaps the most handsome of the buildings erected in the later eighteenth century was the main guard house in the lower close, to the east of the forework gate (78).

This block has a three-arched loggia between two slightly advanced pavilions, and replaced a one-and-a-half storey range projecting at right angles from the forework wall. Nevertheless, in a working barracks there was little room to be sentimental about historic architecture and decoration. Thus, when in 1777 part of the ceiling fell in the royal lodgings of the palace block, it was simply decided to take down the decorative ceilings including those with the portrait roundels known as the Stirling heads (see **44** and **45**). Many of the heads were lost or damaged as a result. In the same spirit the wall-heads of the hall appear to have been simplified by the reduction in height of the crenellated parapet.

Towards the end of the eighteenth century the Napoleonic wars created a need for barrack space within the major Scottish castles on an unprecedented scale, and accommodation within them was strained to its limits. Between March and June 1794, for example, Stirling was the rendezvous for Duncan Campbell of Lochnell's mustering of the Duke of Argyll's Highland regiment. (This was one element of the famous regiment that was to be particularly associated with the later history of the castle, the Argyll and Sutherland Highlanders. The other element was a regiment raised in 1799 by Major General William Wemyss from the estates of the Countess of Sutherland and known as the Sutherland Highlanders, though neither of these regiments was to be permanently housed in the castle until they were united in 1881.)

To meet the new need for provision of barrack beds throughout Scotland, a hasty building campaign was put into effect. At

78 The main guard house.

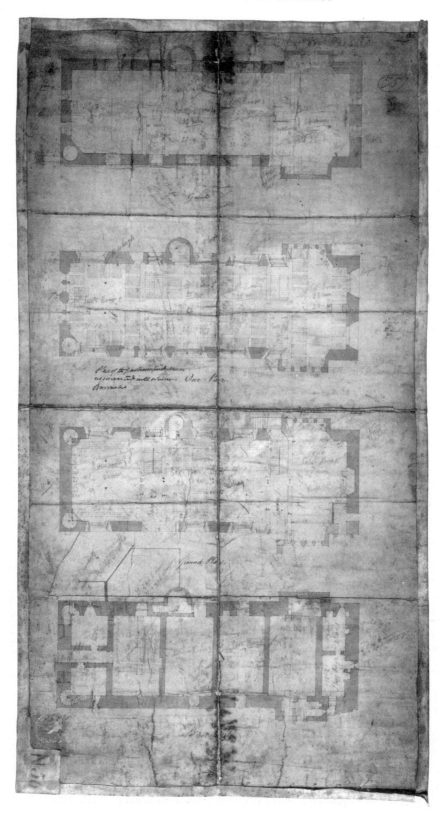

79 *Plans showing the conversion of the great hall into barrack rooms.*

Edinburgh Castle this led to the construction of the vast New Barracks between 1796 and 1799. At Stirling some additional accommodation could be found within the main rooms of the palace, but the main solution was the further subdivision of the great hall to create twelve new barrack rooms (**79**). Two floors were inserted, together with five cross walls and two flights of stairs running the height of the building. In doing this there was no scope to respect historic detail, and any carving or moulding which projected from the wall-face was ruthlessly hacked off. New windows and doorways were cut through the walls while the original openings were blocked or altered beyond recognition (**80, 81**). Most damaging

of all, the hammerbeam roof – which may well have been in a poor state by then – was replaced by a simpler structure which allowed the space of the barrack rooms at attic level to be less impeded.

The early decades of the nineteenth century saw continuing building activity within the castle, and by the central decades of the century plans show the plethora of structures that had spread to meet miltary needs. Within the outer defences, for example, was the barrier guard room with an adjoining prisoner's room on the north side; a straw store (the present shop) faced it across the square and there was an officers' stable and a coach-house to the east. All of these survive in modified form. In

80 *The exterior of the great hall when in use as a barrack block.*

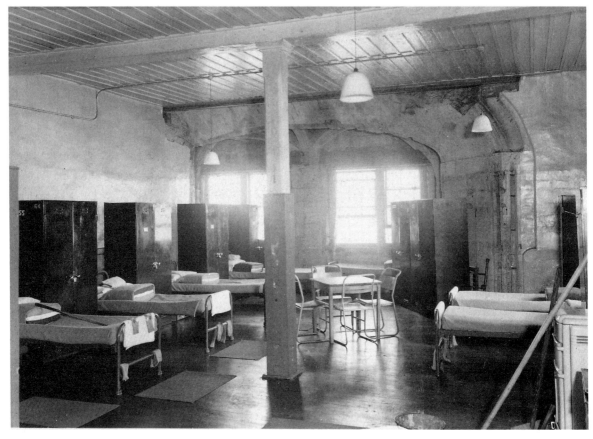

81 *The interior of one of the barrack rooms in the great hall.*

82 *The Fort Major's house.*

83 *The powder magazines in the nether bailey.*

front of the eastern stretch of the forework wall a row of gun sheds had been built, while an engine-house had been added at the north end of the two-storeyed casemates, which themselves had come to be used as contractors' stores. Moving on into the lower close, a pleasingly symmetrical house had been built for the Fort Major next to the main guard house (82). In the nether bailey three powder magazines covered by blast-proof parabolic brick vaults had been constructed in about 1810 (83, 84), with a guard house close to the north gate to watch over them. (This guard house was converted into punishment cells around the 1850s.) Nor did the main buildings of the castle escape further changes, with a cookhouse being added against the west side of the palace,

and an octagonal cistern built within the Lion's Den at its centre. Changes were also made on the approaches to the castle, with a flat area for a parade ground, the present esplanade, being laid out after the acquisition of extra land from the town in 1809. At some stage in the nineteenth century the drawbridge was replaced by one with elaborate cast-iron railings, the appearance of which is recorded in early photographs (85).

In an active garrison it was natural that the architectural needs of the military should have been paramount, and in any case there would then have been little feeling that the historic buildings of the castle were worthy of preservation in their own right. Nevertheless, in some quarters there were already the beginnings of

an appreciation of the castle's fine qualities. As early as 1817 the wife of the deputy governor, Mrs Jane Graham, published *Lacunar Strevelinense*, an invaluable account of the Stirling heads from the palace ceilings, with an engraving showing how the king's outer chamber was thought to have looked when they were in place (see **45**). Before long the castle also started to become something of an attraction for historically minded travellers. Indeed, on 13 September 1849 it was visited by the young Queen Victoria, who felt it was extremely grand, though she confessed that she preferred Edinburgh Castle. Her visit, which was the first by a reigning monarch for 191 years, was commemorated on the parapet of the curtain-wall to the north of the King's Old

84 *The interior of one of the magazines in the nether bailey.*

85 *The last of the drawbridges at the main entrance to the castle.*

86 *The room known as the Douglas Room in the King's Old Building, as remodelled by Robert William Billings (Crown Copyright, Royal Commission on the Ancient and Historical Monuments of Scotland).*

Building, where records of later royal visits have also been inscribed; unfortunately a haze prevented her from seeing the distant hills.

Another visitor at this period was the architect Robert William Billings, who was to include an engraving of the castle in his *Baronial and Ecclesiastical Antiquities of Scotland*, published between 1845 and 1852. This publication was of the greatest importance for making its readers more aware of the qualities of the medieval and Renaissance architecture of Scotland. Billings was given the opportunity to show his own mettle as a historically inspired architect at Stirling shortly afterwards, when the northern end of the King's Old Building was badly damaged by a fire in 1855. This was the part of the building which housed the so-called Douglas Room, from which the body of the murdered

eighth Earl of Douglas was thought to have been ejected in 1452, and it was therefore regarded as of particular historic interest (86). By this stage the building had lost much of its original character as a result of the cutting of new windows to light the inserted floors and subdivided rooms, and little could be done to change this in view of the building's continued use. Nevertheless, in recasing the damaged end of the building Billings did his best to respond to what he could see had been its original character. He heightened the northern end, designing a particularly exuberant façade to overlook the garden on that side of the building (87). He also added a second stair-turret towards the northern end of the courtyard façade, in which the forms of the main stair were closely reflected (see 17).

The castle becomes a monument

It could not be said that Billing's work on the King's Old Building itself marked a complete change in the history of the castle's treatment,

87 The garden front of the King's Old Building as remodelled by Robert William Billings after 1855.

since many of the buildings continued to be adapted to meet the needs of the garrison. Nevertheless, as public awareness of the qualities of the buildings increased, there was a growing sense that more must be done for them. The publication of the first volume of David MacGibbon and Thomas Ross's influential *Castellated and Domestic Architecture of Scotland* in 1887 included reconstruction drawings of how the hall must once have looked, and it can be no coincidence that in 1893 there was a suggestion that it should be restored. Nothing came of this, but the momentum for a new approach to conservation was becoming unstoppable, and the watershed was intervention from a rather unexpected quarter. On 24 September 1906 a letter from the Office of Works to the War Office said that King Edward VII himself was concerned that 'irrevocable damage is being done to Stirling Castle'. It was therefore suggested that responsibility for the fabric of the castle should be transferred to the Office of Works, as had already been done for the Tower of London and Edinburgh Castle; this idea came to fruition at the end of that year.

Of course, some new building continued to be necessary, though this tended to be increasingly limited to less sensitive areas, as when the three magazines in the nether bailey were connected by link buildings in 1908 to form mobilization stores (see **83**). On the part of all concerned, however, there was now a drive to do what was best for the main buildings. In 1911 the Lion's Den at the centre of the palace block was paved more appropriately, while six years later there were works aimed at making the roof of the King's Old Building and the walls of the palace waterproof. On a more ambitious scale, in 1921 the kitchens below the grand battery and the lower storeys of the Elphinstone Tower were excavated, and the stone vaults which once covered them were reinstated (see **29**). In a similar

spirit, in 1925 it was suggested that efforts should be made to recover a number of the Stirling heads from the ceilings of the palace that were held by the Smith Museum in Stirling. Since some of them had only very recently been acquired this was naturally unsuccessful, though the museum eventually generously returned them to the castle in 1970 (see **44**).

Even grander schemes were put forward in the years to either side of the Second World War, and as early as 1911 the Scottish Ecclesiological Society pleaded that the Chapel Royal should be restored. The chapel roof had been repaired in 1708, and in 1887 it was said it had recently been provided with a new roof to shelter the various mundane but necessary functions it housed. By 1911 it contained the soldiers' dining-hall and school, with stores on an inserted upper floor, and restoration was rejected as impracticable. Eight years later Colonel Henderson, the commander of the castle, suggested it should be used as a repository for captured trophies, somewhat to the alarm of the Duke of Montrose, the Lord Lieutenant of Stirlingshire. But the need to treat more appropriately what had once been Scotland's chief place of royal worship was now widely recognized. The idea of restoring it re-emerged in the 1930s, with various designs being drawn up to show how this could be achieved (**88**). As a consequence, the inserted floor and walls were removed, revealing traces of Valentine Jenkin's painted decoration for Charles I in the process (see **54**). However, it was decided that an appeal for funds would be needed, and this was postponed in order to avoid conflict with an appeal for the restoration of Holy Rude parish church. Further works, other than restoration of the paintings, were then prevented by the outbreak of war, and it has only been more recently that work was again initiated.

After the war the idea of restoring the great hall was revived, when Sir Frank Mears of the Scottish War Memorials Advisory Committee suggested in 1946 that this would represent a suitable memorial to the dead. A model was

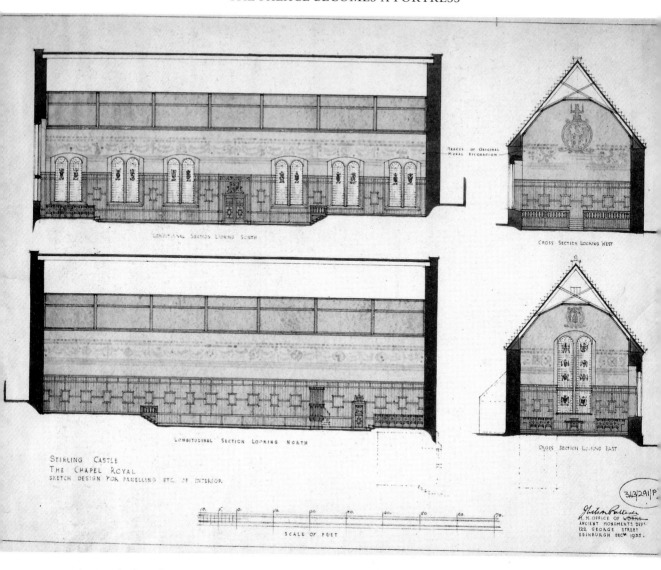

TRACES OF ORIGINAL
MURAL DECORATION

LONGITUDINAL SECTION LOOKING SOUTH

CROSS SECTION LOOKING WEST

LONGITUDINAL SECTION LOOKING NORTH

CROSS SECTION LOOKING EAST

STIRLING CASTLE
THE CHAPEL ROYAL
SKETCH DESIGN FOR PANELLING ETC. OF INTERIOR.

H.M. OFFICE OF WORKS
ANCIENT MONUMENTS DEPT.
122 GEORGE STREET
EDINBURGH DEC. 1935.

SCALE OF FEET

made, and the idea was kept alive for some years, though the need for barrack accommodation within the castle remained an insuperable obstacle. This changed, however, when the castle ceased to function as a military depot in 1964. As a first stage towards determining if the idea might be feasible, parts of the inserted subdivisions were carefully dismantled to see if there was likely to be sufficient evidence to restore the hall authentically. When it became apparent that a combination of the physical evidence of the building itself and the written and drawn evidence of the documentation and survey drawings would allow

88 *Proposals drawn up for the restoration of the Chapel Royal by the Office of Works in 1935.*

89 *The interior of the great hall in course of restoration.*

authoritative restoration to be carried out, it was agreed it should proceed. Work is now well advanced, and it is possible to see how the hall will look when it has reverted to its early sixteenth-century state (**89, colour plate 9**).

But work in recent years has not been limited to the great hall. Although Historic Scotland and its predecessor bodies have always seen their main role as preserving the

architectural and archaeological remains of Scotland's past as they have come down to us, so that the information they embody can be handed on to future generations with as little disturbance as possible, it is recognized that Stirling Castle is in a category of its own. While the later changes to its great buildings are certainly an important aspect of the castle's continuing history as a fortress, few would deny that the buildings lost part of the character originally intended for them in the process. It has therefore been accepted that, where there is sufficient evidence for judicious restoration, consideration will be given to doing this. Consequently, in the greater part of the royal lodgings of the palace works are in progress that will give back to them much of their first appearance. By contrast, the evidence for the forework and the King's Old Building is insufficiently complete for us to be entirely certain about all of their original details, and in such cases restoration could not be justified.

With all this work in progress, Stirling Castle is a particularly fascinating place to visit. There are times, indeed, that one suspects it cannot look very different from how it must have done during so much of the reigns of James IV and James V, when many of its great buildings were under construction.

CHAPTER FIVE

Buildings in the vicinity of Stirling Castle

Stirling is additionally fortunate in that several other medieval and Renaissance buildings survive in and around the town, since this makes it easier to understand how a major royal castle was at the hub of a diverse range of functions and activities. This book ends with a brief discussion of some of the most important of them, though it must be remembered there were once many other such buildings. Among these were religious houses for the Dominican and Observant Franciscan friars, perhaps as many as five medieval hospitals, and several residences of the nobility. There are also surviving fragments of the defensive wall which extended down from the castle to protect the more vulnerable south and west sides of the burgh and which, in their present fragmentary form, date mainly from a decision taken by the Burgh Council in 1547 at a time when an English attack was feared. Among several other buildings which also deserve to be seen by those with an interest in historic architecture are the Town House and Cowane's Hospital, the latter being a seventeenth-century almshouse. However, the buildings that have been picked out for discussion here are those which had a particular relationship with the castle, either because they were built under the patronage of the kings who lived in the castle, or because they came into existence because of the proximity of the castle.

Stirling bridge

The crossing of the Forth at this point of the river was always one of the most important reasons for Stirling's existence and development, and it is likely there was a bridge here from as soon as its construction was technically feasible. It seems, however, that the earlier bridges may have been in a slightly different position from the one we now see, because in 1905 foundations were observed of a timber bridge 60m (197ft) upstream. There was certainly a bridge of some sort by the mid-thirteenth century, since it is referred to on at least three maps, and its representation on the burgh seal by 1296 shows that its existence was regarded as a particular reason for pride. The bridge was to be of crucial importance in the following year, when its narrowness, which permitted only two horsemen to ride abreast of each other, helped the Scottish patriots Andrew Murray and William Wallace to defeat the English forces at the battle which took its name from the bridge (a battle commemorated by the Wallace Monument, **colour plate 10**). At that time it was still of timber, and it was apparently broken down as one consequence the battle. A timber bridge was, by its nature, always more at risk than one of masonry from the effects either of enemy action or of flooding, and there seem to have been several periods when the only way of crossing the river was by boat, suggesting that the bridge was down at those times.

90 *Stirling bridge.*

It is uncertain when a stone bridge was first built. One possibility is the early fifteenth century, when the pope agreed that indulgences could be offered to those who contributed to the work, reminding us that the construction of bridges to assist the movements of pilgrims and merchants was always regarded as a meritorious work of charity. Payments were being made towards construction in 1408 and 1415.

However, the existing bridge looks later than that, and is perhaps more likely to date from the later years of the fifteenth century (**90, colour plate 11**). It is an impressive structure of four arches, the largest having a span of over 17m (55ft) and rising 11.5m (37ft) above water-level. The carriageway is nearly 4.5m

91 *A late seventeenth-century drawing by John Slezer of the castle and bridge, showing the gate-houses on the bridge (Public Record Office).*

(15ft) wide, and until the eighteenth century it was defended by three gatehouses, one at each end and one over the central pier (**91**). There has inevitably been much rebuilding at various times in the bridge's history. The most extensive operation was after one of its arches was cut in 1745 in an attempt to stop the troops of Bonnie Prince Charlie entering the town on his southward march.

Parish church of the Holy Rude

It may be that the first place of worship in Stirling was within the castle and, as we have seen, a chapel there was certainly built, or rebuilt, in the time of Alexander I (1107–24). It is likely to have been David I (1124–53) who founded a church in the town which grew up at the gates of the castle, since we know that David was keen to ensure that the spiritual needs of his people were properly met by the provision of parish churches in all parts of the kingdom. This possibility gains support from the fact that in about 1150 David confirmed to his abbey at Dunfermline the possession of two churches in Stirling. But nothing remains of that period because the town's church was reconstructed in the later Middle Ages as one of the grandest in Scotland, at a time when several of the greater burghs were rebuilding their churches as the main focus of their civic pride.

The date when this rebuilding started at Stirling is not entirely certain. The church is said to have been destroyed in a fire of around 1414 and provision was being made for some work soon afterwards. But all the evidence points to the main campaign of rebuilding being rather later than that, the catalyst to action perhaps being destruction resulting from the riots which followed James II's killing of the eighth Earl of Douglas in 1452. Rebuilding was carried out in two main phases, reflecting the fact that there was always separate financial responsibility for the two parts of a parish church. The first phase covered the nave and the lower part of the western tower; these were

92 *The nave and west tower of Holy Rude parish church.*

the parts which were the responsibility of the burgh. The second phase covered the chancel; that was the responsibility of Dunfermline Abbey, to which the parish, and thus much of its income, had been granted. But it is a clear sign of how important their church was to the burgesses of Stirling that in 1507 they agreed to carry out rebuilding of the chancel themselves, in return for certain concessions from Dunfermline Abbey.

The result of these two phases of building is a magnificent structure which looks particularly impressive from the east, as seen by those approaching the castle up the steep St John Street (**92, 93, colour plate 12**). The nave is of five bays, with stone-vaulted aisles and a two-storeyed central space covered by an open-timber tie-beam roof. A number of chapels are known to have been added against the aisles to house chantry chapels, where prayers could

93 *The parish church of the Holy Rude engraved for Francis Grose (*Antiquities of Scotland, *1789–91).*

be said for the souls of their founders, though only one of those now survives complete. At the west end is a bell-tower, though it was raised no higher than the level of the main nave roof at this first stage of rebuilding operations.

The chancel, which was presumably started soon after the agreement with Dunfermline of 1507, was of only three bays in length, but was in fact planned on an even more ambitious scale than had been the nave. It was to have been separated from the nave by transepts (cross arms), with a second tower above them, a most unusual arrangement for which the only known Scottish parallel would have been the twelfth-century work at Kelso Abbey. The east end of the chancel terminated in a great polygonal apse as the setting for the high altar. It is possible that the main space of the chancel was planned to be three storeys high. The evidence for this possibility is the way in which the present upper storey seems to have been intended as a triforium, with arches opening into the space between the vaults and roofs over the aisles, rather than as the row of upper windows known as a clerestorey. It therefore appears that a clerestorey could have been intended above this. In adopting such a design the master mason may have been inspired by the slightly earlier nave of Linlithgow church, adjacent to the royal palace there, which had also been given three storeys. As part of this later operation the western tower of the nave was completed by the addition of a high superstructure, and it seems there were also plans to add a third storey over the nave from the evidence of the higher roof mouldings that were built in with the tower.

In fact this grandiose scheme was never completed. No third storey was ever built over either the nave or chancel, nor was a central tower built. The transepts were only eventually completed in a restoration of the 1930s when the architect James Miller also removed the wall which had divided the church into two parts since 1656. Nevertheless, even in its incomplete state the church is one of the largest of the late medieval burgh churches. Construction was probably largely complete by the 1540s when the clergy who served in the church were brought together within an incorporation known as a college, under the leadership of the vicar. This allowed the services to be carried out with the greatest dignity, in a way that almost rivalled the religious observances of the cathedrals, and to the great enrichment of the spiritual life of the burgh. It was clearly regarded as a suitable setting for the coronation of the infant James VI in 1567.

Cambuskenneth Abbey

David I was a particularly open-handed patron of the church. As well as encouraging both the setting up of a network of parishes and the reorganization of the system of bishops' dioceses, he was a great friend of the religious orders, and introduced several new ones to Scotland. A number of the orders were given homes close to the main royal residences, suggesting that David intended to take a continuing interest in them. In the valley of the Forth to the east of Stirling – and in a relationship to the castle comparable to that which Holyrood Abbey had with Edinburgh Castle – David established an abbey of Arrouaisian Canons. This order of priests living a form of monastic life had been founded very recently by Abbot Gervase at Arrouaise in north-east France; it was a branch of the Augustinian Canons, but aimed to follow a particularly austere form of life. The abbey was probably established in about 1140 when we know that David was making endowments to Arrouaise itself, though it seems that the canons eventually came to regard themselves simply as Augustinian.

As might be expected with an abbey so close to one of the main royal residences, it played an important role in the history of the kingdom. We know, for example, that a number of parliaments were held there, one of the most important being that of 1314, when those who had fought against Robert I at Bannockburn were deprived of their Scottish estates if they had not since been reconciled. It was also the burial place of James III after he had been killed at the battle of Sauchieburn in 1488, where the tomb must have been a constant reminder to James IV of the part he had played in his own father's death.

However, very little of either the abbey church or the monastic buildings has survived, though parts of their lower walls were rather crudely excavated in 1864 and subsequently consolidated to allow them to be seen. The most complete single feature is the bell-tower which still stands entire, partly as a result of heavy restoration (**94, colour plate 13**). It was

94 *The bell- tower of Cambuskenneth Abbey.*

always a free-standing structure, set a short distance to the north-west of the abbey church. The church itself, on the evidence of its excavated lower walls, seems to have been built around the early years of the thirteenth century. At the east end was a rectangular presbytery for the high altar, which was flanked on each side by transepts (cross arms), with a pair of chapels on the east side of each. There may have been a low tower over the junction of the transepts with the main body of the church, since in 1378 it was said that a tower had been struck by lightning with consequent damage to the choir. West of this was the nave, which had the canons' choir in the part closest to the presbytery. The nave seems originally to have been without aisles, though one was added later, on the north side, which was the side away from the cloister. The west doorway, which was the main processional entrance to the church,

stands largely complete, having been brought into modified service as the gateway to a later graveyard within the western bays of the nave.

The cloister was in the preferred position on the south side of the nave, and fragmentary remains of the canons' domestic quarters which extended around its three other sides may be seen. On the south are the footings of the refectory, while the chapter house, the principal meeting-room of the abbey, is the main room of which there are traces on the east. A short distance to the east and south-east of this nucleus of buildings are a number of other buildings, near the bank of the Forth. The purpose of these is unknown, though it is possible one was a new abbot's house referred to in 1520. One of the later abbots of Cambuskenneth was Alexander Myln, the first president of James V's college of

95 *Mar's Work.*

justice, who also breathed new life and enthusiasm into his community of canons.

Mar's Work

This was the town house of John, the first Earl of Mar of the Erskine family (see **49**). Mar had a highly eventful career in the reigns of Mary Queen of Scots and James VI, holding Edinburgh Castle at the time of the upheavals of the Reformation in 1559–60. He was created Earl of Mar in 1565, and in the following year Mary made him hereditary keeper of Stirling Castle, an office which many of his predecessors had already held on a non-hereditary basis. This was to be a position of particular importance because it meant that he had custody of the young James VI following the abdication of his mother in 1567. He reached the height of his power in the last years of his life when, from September 1571 until his death in the castle in October 1572, he was Regent of Scotland, and he was the only one of James VI's regents to die peacefully in his bed.

The main residence of the earl's family was a few miles away at Alloa, but it was clearly important to him to have another near the royal castle of which he was keeper. His new house was set in a dominating position to the north-east of Holy Rude church, and at the head of Stirling's main market area of Broad Street. From dated stones it seems it was started in 1570. In the years leading up to the Reformation the Erskine family had acquired control of the Augustinian monasteries of Cambuskenneth and Inchmahome, and of the Premonstratensian abbey of Dryburgh in the Borders. Not only was a handsome income derived from those, but there is a tradition that the buildings of Cambuskenneth were robbed to find building materials for his new house at Stirling. A number of reused stones from some ecclesiastical building are certainly to be seen, including an incised consecration cross, though some of them could equally have come from other religious buildings within the burgh.

96 A heraldic panel on Mar's Work.

Mar's house was probably never completed, but it seems to have been planned as a quadrangular structure around a central courtyard. The main front overlooked Broad Street, and was originally three storeys in height (**95, 96, colour plate 14**). At the centre of this front was a gateway, flanked by semi-octagonal towers, which gave access to the courtyard behind. To either side of this gate were vaulted basements. The fact that each had a doorway and a window towards the street suggests they could have been used as shops, a use which was not as inconsistent with such a grand town house as might first appear from what we know of houses of comparable scale on the Continent. The main rooms were on the first floor, and there were presumably chambers in an attic storey above. The decoration of this façade represents a particularly important early phase of Renaissance design in Scotland. In its details there was evidently some influence from the palace in the castle of thirty years

97 Argyll's Lodging.

earlier (see **38**). This is seen particularly in the strong horizontal string course below the first-floor windows, the vertical division of the main floor by baluster shafts carrying figures, and the setting of the windows in panels projected out from the main wall surface. The heraldic and figurative carving deserves close inspection, the latter including what appears to be a female corpse in a winding-sheet!

Argyll's Lodging

Argyll's Lodging is one of the most delightful buildings in Stirling, and gives an impressive sense of architectural homogeneity despite the fact that it only reached its present state after several phases of development. It now consists of three ranges grouped around a courtyard

that is entered through a screen wall on its west side, and the end result is perhaps more like something that might be expected in a French provincial town than a building in central Scotland (**97, colour plate 15**). The earliest part of the house was probably a two-storeyed block which is now submerged within the east end of the north wing. Only a kitchen and two vaulted cellars survive of this, but from what we know of similar houses elsewhere it probably had a hall and chamber as the owner's own lodging on the first floor. This part of the house is likely to date from the sixteenth century, though there are signs that it was both enlarged and heightened later in that century. Yet further extensions in the form of a kitchen wing were also added to the west of the original block.

These earliest parts of the building were absorbed within two phases of later rebuilding that are datable to the 1630s and 1670s. Both of those periods were highly significant for Scotland's royal history. It was in 1633 that Charles I at last made his belated 'homecoming' to his northern kingdom, while in the 1670s there were hopes that Charles II would come north more often at a time when he had agreed, a little reluctantly, to the rebuilding of his palace at Holyrood. At both dates it must therefore have seemed likely that Stirling was about to come into its own again as an important royal residence, and by some at least of Scotland's nobility it must have been thought politic to ensure that they were well housed in the vicinity of the castle.

The two phases of later building were the work of different people. In about 1630 the house had been acquired by William Alexander, Viscount Stirling, who was to be created Earl of Stirling and Viscount Canada in 1633 (98). Stirling was an accomplished courtier, and was the prime mover behind the attempted colonization of Nova Scotia, which had been granted to him in 1621. His additions to his house at Stirling consisted of a three-storeyed range, running north–south at right angles to the original block, and with a second block at its southern end to balance the earlier building. The main rooms within these extensions were probably an entrance hall and stair hall on the ground floor, and a great chamber on the first floor; there was probably a state apartment in the wing at its southern end, and additional bedchambers throughout the top floor. The date 1632 was carved on the porch which covers the entrance from the courtyard, although that porch has evidently been brought from another part of the building since it does not fit very well in its present position. All of this new work was embellished with fine carving to the windows and fireplaces, much of which is so closely related to details of Heriot's Hospital in Edinburgh that it seems possible the master mason William Ayton could have had a hand in the work.

In the 1660s the house was bought by the ninth Earl of Argyll, who eventually set about

98 *The Earl of Stirling.*

further rebuilding, as well as remodelling what was already there. As part of this work he extended the south wing to the same length as that on the north, and embellished the screen wall across the entrance to the courtyard with a handsome Classical entrance archway at its centre. He also extended his additions southwards along the street front to provide a considerable amount of extra accommodation, though those southward extensions were largely demolished in the 1860s (99). In making his additions Argyll was careful to make his new work sit comfortably with what had already been built. The details of his work, however, were more severely Classical than those of the Earl of Stirling, as might be expected at a period when 'correctness' in Classical architecture was coming to be more assiduously cultivated. Whereas the work of the 1630s had highly enriched strapwork gablets to the windows and armorial panel, Argyll's work has simpler curved triangular or

99 *Argyll's Lodging, showing the street front before the demolition of its southern end* (J. Ronald, The Story of the Argyle Lodging).

100 *Decorative painted arcading in the high dining room of Argyll's Lodging.*

segmental pediments, that at the base of one of the stair-turrets bearing the date 1674. A particularly fine feature is the painted decoration in the first-floor high dining-room (100).

The house remained in the ownership of the Earls and Dukes of Argyll until 1764, since when it has been put to a number of uses. In about 1800 it was acquired by the crown, at a time when the castle was being modified to make it more suitable for use by a permanent garrison, and for many years it served as the military hospital. More recently it has also served as a youth hostel, and many visitors to Scotland have fond memories of discovering some of the building's more unexpected qualities while staying there. Currently, as an extension to the improvements that are being carried out within the castle itself, the main rooms are being refurbished in a way that will allow them to be seen much as they would have been in the seventeenth century. The rest of the house is now used as an institute for international Scottish studies by Stirling University.

Further reading

Much of the documentation relating to the castle is to be found in the published Exchequer Rolls and the accounts of the Lord High Treasurer and of the Masters of Works.

The most valuable description and architectural analysis of the castle and of the other buildings in the burgh is in the first volume of the Stirlingshire *Inventory* of the Royal Commission on the Ancient and Historical Monuments of Scotland (Edinburgh, 1963).

Among the many other publications containing information relating to the castle the following books or articles are particularly important:

Graham, Jane *Lacunar Strevelinense*, Edinburgh, 1817.

Stair-Kerr, Eric *Stirling Castle*, 2nd edn, Stirling, 1928.

Crawford, H.J. 'Stirling Castle in art', *Transactions of the Stirlingshire Natural History Association*, 1934–5.

Dunbar, John *The Stirling heads*, 2nd edn, Edinburgh, 1975.

Barrow, G.W.S. *Robert Bruce*, Edinburgh, 1976.

Ewart, Gordon 'Excavations at Stirling Castle 1977–78', *Post-medieval archaeology*, vol. 14, 1980.

Lynch, Michael 'Queen Mary's triumph: the baptismal celebrations at Stirling in December 1566', *Scottish Historical Review*, vol. 69, 1990.

Index

(Page numbers in **bold** refer to illustrations)